Work and Play

P9-CAO-783

Program Authors

Connie Juel, Ph.D.

Jeanne R. Paratore, Ed.D.

Deborah Simmons, Ph.D.

Sharon Vaughn, Ph.D.

ISBN: 0-328-21517-1
Copyright © 2008 Pearson Education, Inc.

11 12 13 V011 12 11 10 09
CC1

PEARSON
Scott
Foresman

Editorial Offices: Glenview, Illinois • Parsippany, New Jersey • New York, New York
Sales Offices: Boston, Massachusetts • Duluth, Georgia • Glenview, Illinois
Coppell, Texas • Sacramento, California • Mesa, Arizona

UNIT 2 Contents

Work and Play

NEW IDEAS

How can we use our talents to help others?

WORKING TOGETHER

How can we work together to achieve a goal?

NEW IDEAS

Contents

NEW IDEAS

Words 2 the Wise

People don't learn only by studying textbooks in school. This week you'll explore **new ideas**. As you read, think about how you can learn outside of the classroom.

OTHER WAYS OF LEARNING

Whenever we share our knowledge with other people, we end up learning too! Are you good at chess? Why not teach someone else how to play? You will be learning at the same time.

Are you good at playing soccer? Why not share that talent with someone who needs some tips on playing? When you teach someone else how to kick or pass, you explain it step-by-step. Answering questions about your sport will help you learn more about it. You will also learn more about your teammates.

9

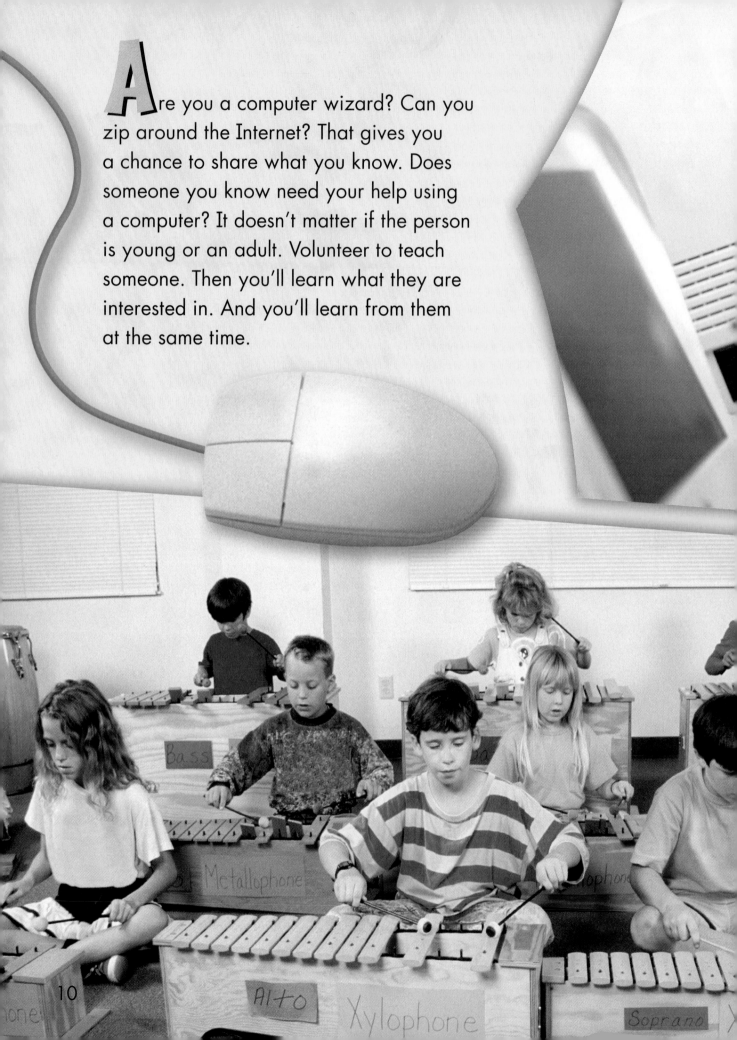

Are you a computer wizard? Can you zip around the Internet? That gives you a chance to share what you know. Does someone you know need your help using a computer? It doesn't matter if the person is young or an adult. Volunteer to teach someone. Then you'll learn what they are interested in. And you'll learn from them at the same time.

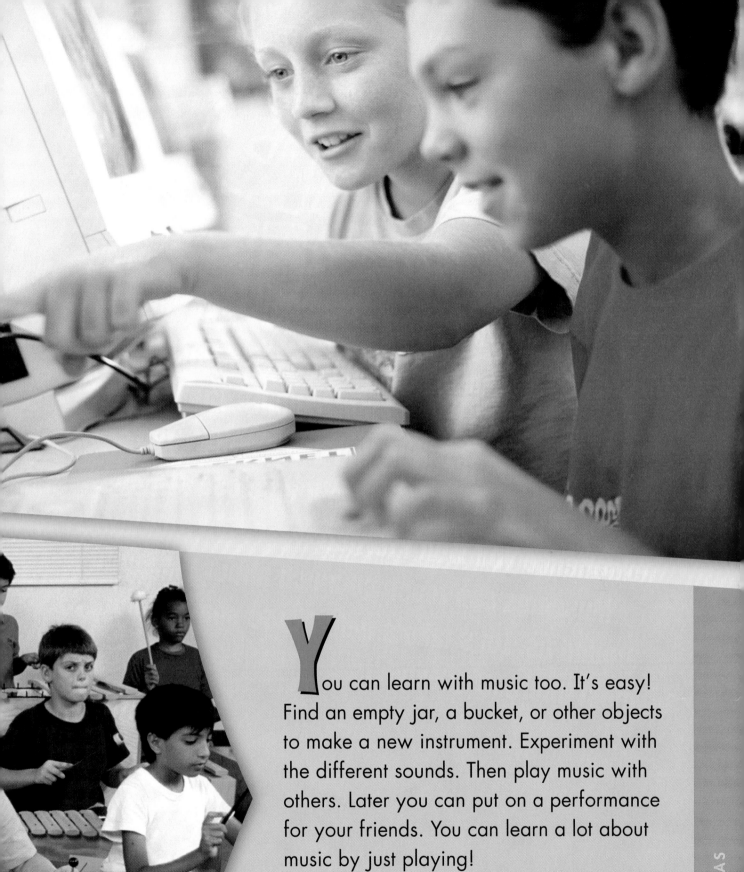

Y ou can learn with music too. It's easy! Find an empty jar, a bucket, or other objects to make a new instrument. Experiment with the different sounds. Then play music with others. Later you can put on a performance for your friends. You can learn a lot about music by just playing!

As you can see, teaching and learning go hand in hand.

phone

by Julie Lavender

FIELD TRIPS

Have you been to a museum lately? Have you ever seen an interactive exhibit? That means you can touch it. You can smell it. You can hear it. And you can see it up close. It's an experience you won't forget!

Museums can teach so much about the world around us. Let's take a field trip to some of our most interesting exhibits.

At some museums you can experience many of the same challenges as astronauts.

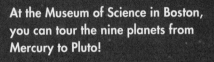

At the Museum of Science in Boston, you can tour the nine planets from Mercury to Pluto!

WHERE ARE YOU?

Do you like space? You can explore the universe at the Museum of Science in Boston, Massachusetts. It has a large-scale model of our solar system. It extends nine miles! You can see how big our solar system really is.

Do you like looking at the stars? On Friday nights, the museum staff will teach you how to use a telescope. Find out what's really going on out there.

A STORM'S COMING!

Is it going to rain? Meteorologists (MEE-tee-uh-ROL-uh-jists) predict the weather. They study weather patterns. They use weather instruments. And they look at satellite photos of the Earth.

You can be a meteorologist too at Discovery Place. It is in North Carolina. They have lots of weather exhibits. You can touch a tornado. You can learn to read radar. You can be a meteorologist in a TV studio.

There are about 800 tornadoes every year in the United States.

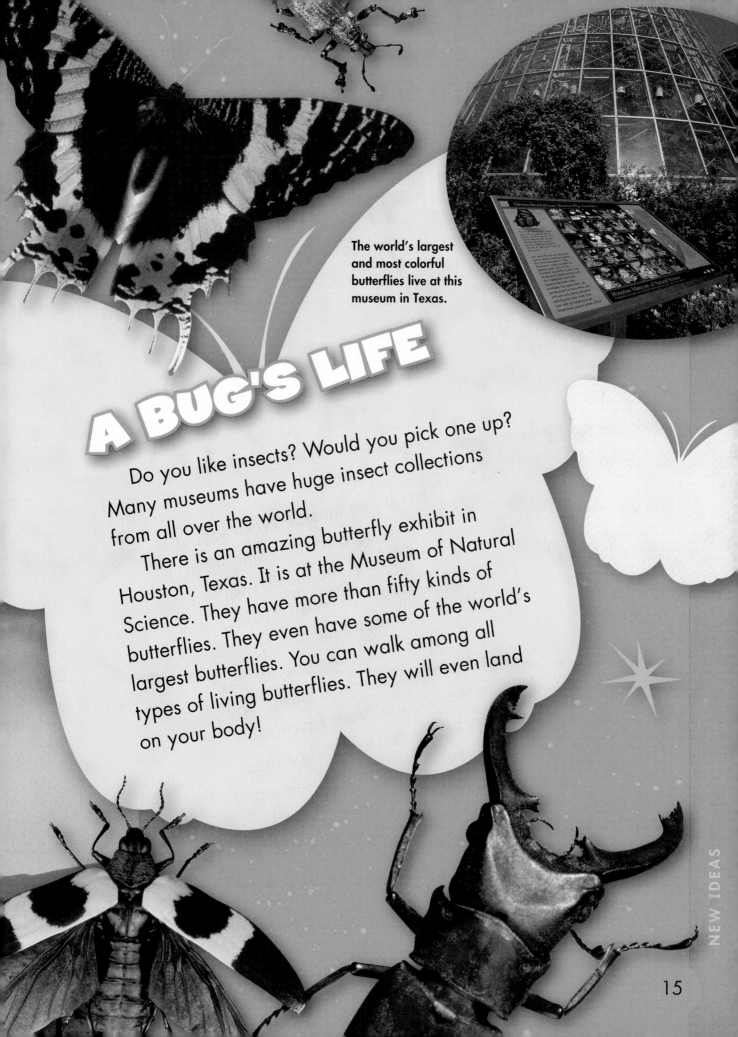

The world's largest and most colorful butterflies live at this museum in Texas.

A BUG'S LIFE

Do you like insects? Would you pick one up? Many museums have huge insect collections from all over the world.

There is an amazing butterfly exhibit in Houston, Texas. It is at the Museum of Natural Science. They have more than fifty kinds of butterflies. They even have some of the world's largest butterflies. You can walk among all types of living butterflies. They will even land on your body!

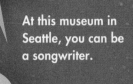
At this museum in Seattle, you can be a songwriter.

LIVE FROM SEATTLE!

Do you like music? What would it be like to be a famous singer? You can learn about the music business at the Experience Music Project. It is in Seattle, Washington.

The museum takes you through the history of modern music. You can learn about your favorite singers. You can see the clothes that they wore. You can see many of the instruments they played. You can even play instruments.

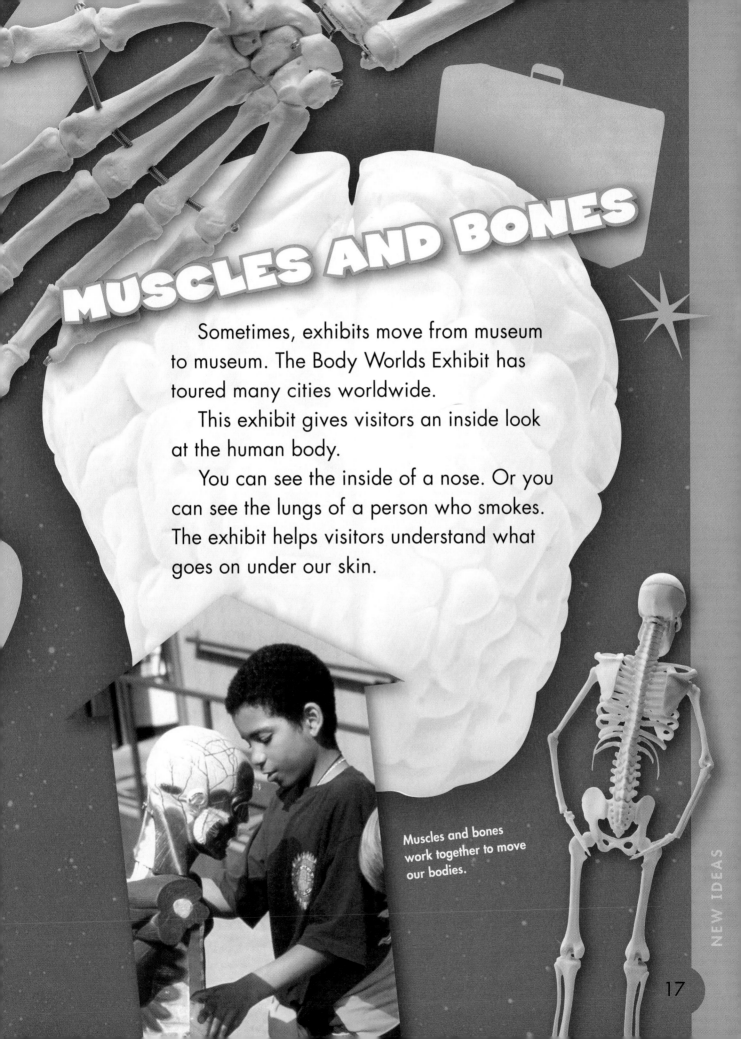

MUSCLES AND BONES

Sometimes, exhibits move from museum to museum. The Body Worlds Exhibit has toured many cities worldwide.

This exhibit gives visitors an inside look at the human body.

You can see the inside of a nose. Or you can see the lungs of a person who smokes. The exhibit helps visitors understand what goes on under our skin.

Muscles and bones work together to move our bodies.

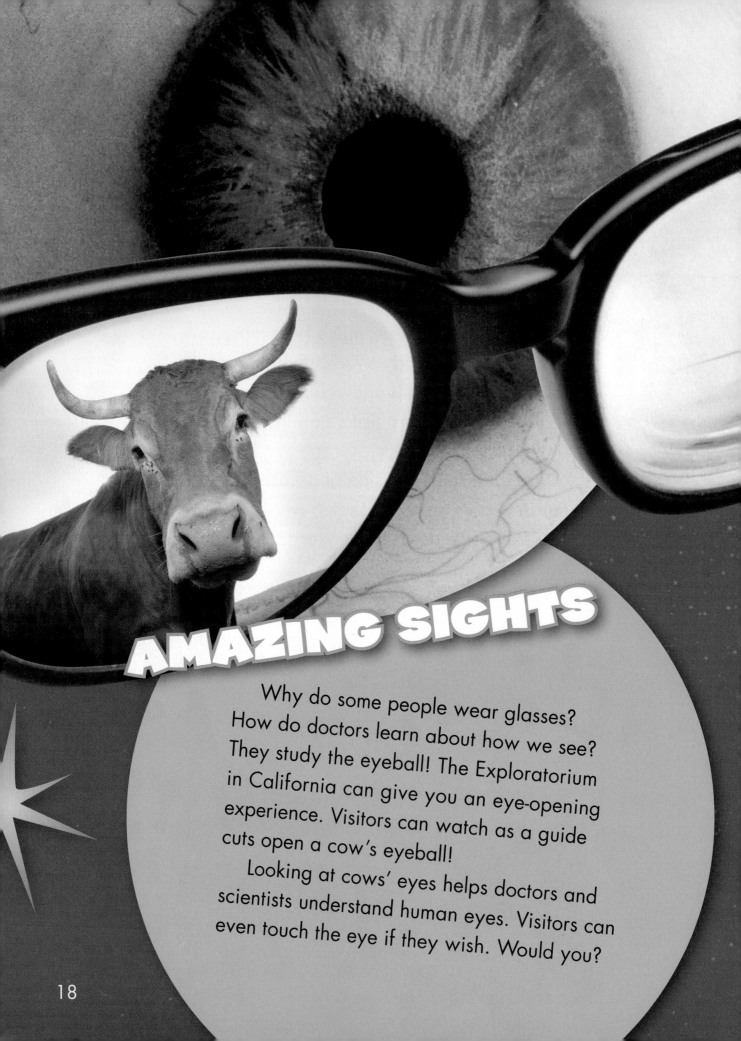

AMAZING SIGHTS

Why do some people wear glasses? How do doctors learn about how we see? They study the eyeball! The Exploratorium in California can give you an eye-opening experience. Visitors can watch as a guide cuts open a cow's eyeball!

Looking at cows' eyes helps doctors and scientists understand human eyes. Visitors can even touch the eye if they wish. Would you?

Have you enjoyed our field trip? Interactive museums can teach us new things by using all of our senses.

Are there museums in your community? Maybe they have some exhibits that can help you learn about our world. They can also inspire you to explore the universe!

WHAT DO YOU THINK?

What is one way learning at a museum is different from learning in a classroom?

The BEAST in Grandpa's House

by Daniel Schafer
illustrated by Jeff Mangiat

"Maria!" Grandpa Alex said as he opened the door. "Right on time."

Our chess set was on the kitchen table. Grandpa and I play chess every Saturday. But the game would have to wait. Today Grandpa Alex needed my help.

"The beast is waiting in the living room," Grandpa warned.

I laughed. "Mom said you're learning about computers to widen your horizons. But you once said 'Human brains are better than computer brains.' What happened?" I asked.

"The Chess Club made me secretary. I said I'd communicate by e-mail," he told me.

"But you don't know how to use a computer," I said.

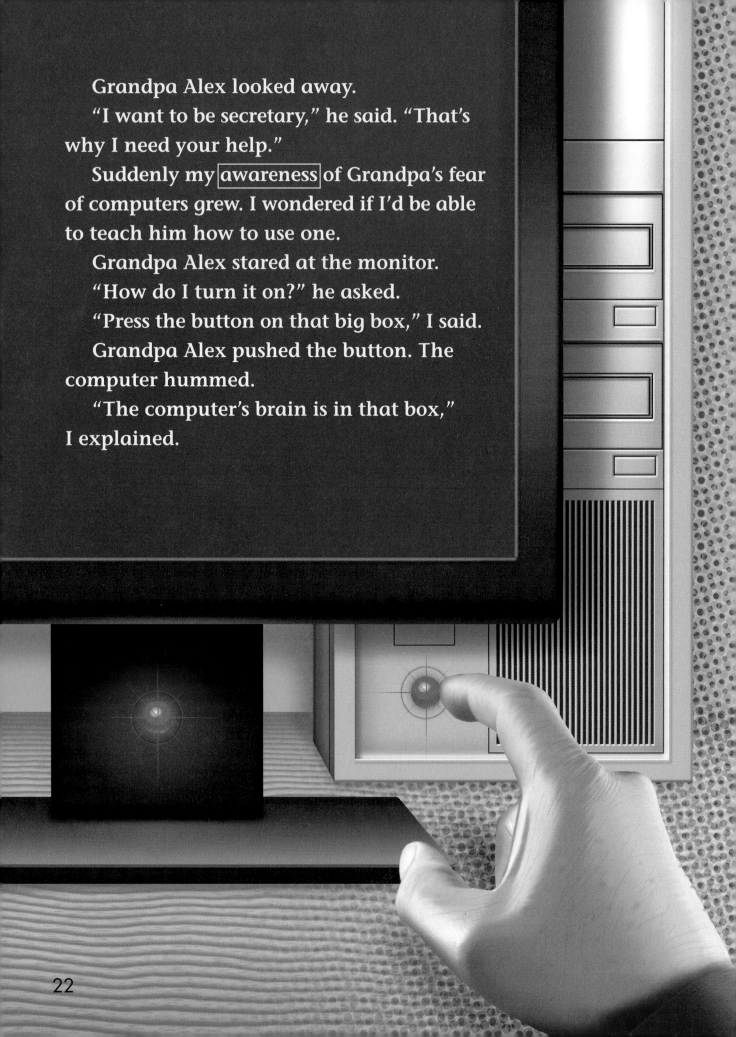

Grandpa Alex looked away.

"I want to be secretary," he said. "That's why I need your help."

Suddenly my awareness of Grandpa's fear of computers grew. I wondered if I'd be able to teach him how to use one.

Grandpa Alex stared at the monitor.

"How do I turn it on?" he asked.

"Press the button on that big box," I said.

Grandpa Alex pushed the button. The computer hummed.

"The computer's brain is in that box," I explained.

Grandpa Alex looked confused.

"Let's log onto the Internet," I said. "Move your mouse to the picture of the eye on your screen."

"Does the mouse bite?" he joked.

"It hasn't bitten me yet," I replied as I helped him move it. "Slide your mouse around. See how the arrow moves on the screen?"

The arrow reached the eye picture.

"Click the button," I said. "Now put the arrow on the e-mail menu."

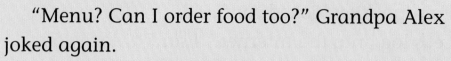

"Menu? Can I order food too?" Grandpa Alex joked again.

"A menu is a list of things the computer can do. It's like a restaurant menu," I explained.

Grandpa nodded and moved the mouse. The arrow darted all over the screen. He frowned.

"I can't comprehend this!" he exclaimed.

"Try again," I said. "Move the mouse slowly until you are used to it."

Grandpa moved the mouse. The arrow moved across the screen again. I put my hand over his hand and helped him move the mouse to the e-mail menu.

"Now click the button on the mouse," I said. Grandpa clumsily hit the button. The mouse moved away. Another program on the computer opened on the screen.

"What happened?" Grandpa Alex asked.

"You opened a window by mistake," I said.

"I'm not near any windows!" Grandpa said.

"Windows are the boxes that open on the screen,"
I said. It was hard for him to comprehend this.

"I'll never learn to use a computer," he said.

Then I remembered when I learned about fractions
in math class. I felt confused and wanted to quit too.
My awareness of how Grandpa felt grew.

"If I can learn fractions," I told him, "you can do this."

"Okay. I'll try again," he said. "Wait. What is this button?"

He pointed to a picture of a chessboard on the screen.

"You can also play games on the computer," I said.

I was surprised when Grandpa Alex clicked the mouse on the chessboard by himself. The game opened.

"Maria," he said, "e-mail can wait. Today, you can widen my horizons by teaching me how to play chess on the computer!"

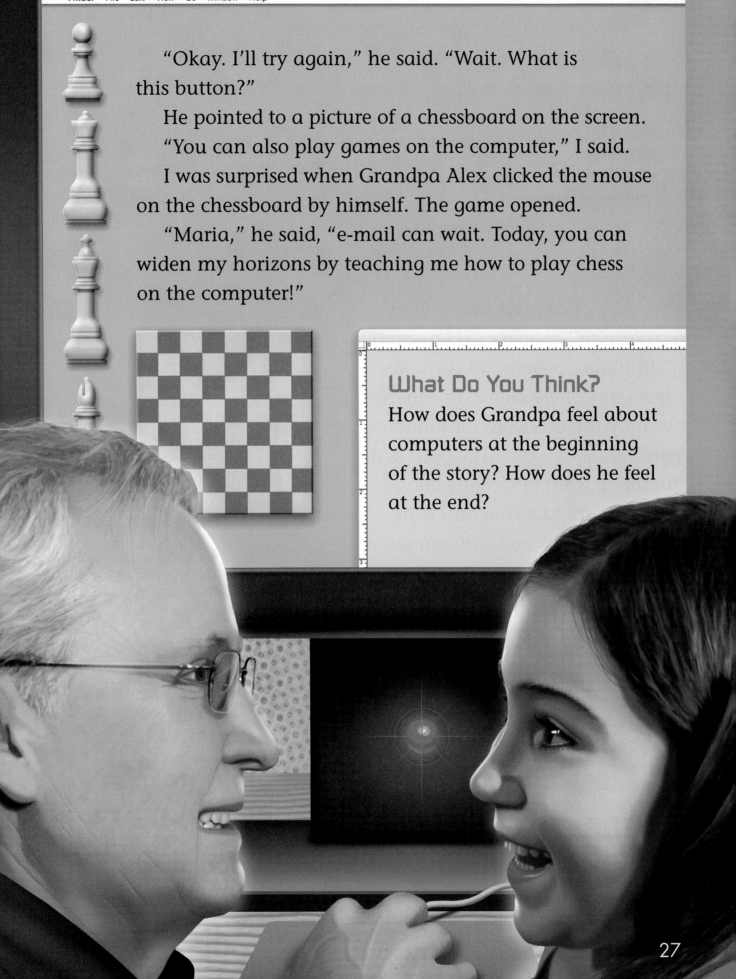

What Do You Think?

How does Grandpa feel about computers at the beginning of the story? How does he feel at the end?

27

Japanese Cartoons

Cartoons from Japan are called *anime* (AH-nee-may). In Japan, people call cartoons from anywhere *anime*. In America, we only use this word for Japanese cartoons. *Manga* (MAHN-gah) is the Japanese word for "comic book." Anime programs are on TV. In Japan, adults and children enjoy anime programs.

In Japan, comic books are called manga.

Spot on: Kanjl, Niragana, Katagana

manga POWER

Nr. 19/2003
Deutschland
€ 5,-

Peach Girl

RAVE

Kaito Saint Tail

Taiyo no Ijiwaru

Anime is unique for its style of drawing characters. Anime programs are similar to cartoons on TV.

Each year, children and adults attend a two-day International Anime Fair. Fans of anime can see the latest manga and meet the artists who draw them. They can even watch anime in 3-D.

3D Hi-Vision

These kids are wearing special glasses to watch animation in 3-D.

4 You 2 Do

Word Play

The word awareness has two parts:
aware + *ness*. You can add the ending
–ness to many words. Add the ending
–ness to the words below. What are
the new words? What do they mean?

gentle   fair   good

Find other words that you can
add the *–ness* to.

Making Connections

Museums share knowledge
about a variety of things.
What might Grandpa Alex
want to learn at a museum?

On Paper

What type of museum would
you like to visit? Write about
the items that would be on
display in a special exhibit.

Answers for Word Play: gentleness, fairness, goodness

WORKING TOGETHER

Contents

WORKING TOGETHER

Words 2 the Wise

This week you'll explore how people are **working together.** As you read, think about a time when you worked with others to achieve a goal.

TEAM

Working together gets the job done.

A construction crew raises a frame. Men and women shout out to one another. "Turn it!" "Lift!" "Pull!"

A quarterback gathers his team. He calls the play. Everyone needs to be in place. Everyone needs to know what to do.

WORK

Someone calls a reporter with breaking news. The reporter goes to the scene. He writes his article and sends it to the printer. Thousands of copies of the next day's paper are printed. A delivery person brings the daily newspaper to your front door.

What do all these people have in common? They use teamwork to get the job done.

It takes a team of people to make the newspapers you see every day.

35

All Together

by Marcus Wheeler

The conductor stands up. The musicians watch him closely. He lifts his arm. They lift their instruments. They are ready to play.

He sweeps his right hand down. The music begins. His left arm tells the musicians how to play. The music can be loud or soft. Or it can be slow or fast. Music fills the air. This is an orchestra.

The musicians in an orchestra wait for the conductor's signal to begin playing.

Now

An orchestra is a large group of musicians. It often plays classical music. A big orchestra can have 100 musicians! An orchestra needs collaboration. This is when the musicians and the conductor work together. This takes practice, practice, practice.

Musicians in an orchestra sit in sections. Each section has its own type of instrument.

strings

woodwinds

brass

percussion

Violins are stringed instruments that come in many different sizes.

Parts of an Orchestra

An orchestra has four sections. There are the strings, the woodwinds, the brass, and the percussion.

The strings section includes violins, violas, cellos, and double basses. Stringed instruments are played with a bow.

The woodwind section includes flutes, oboes, clarinets, and bassoons. They are called woodwinds because they used to be made out of wood. Now some are made out of metal.

woodwind

strings

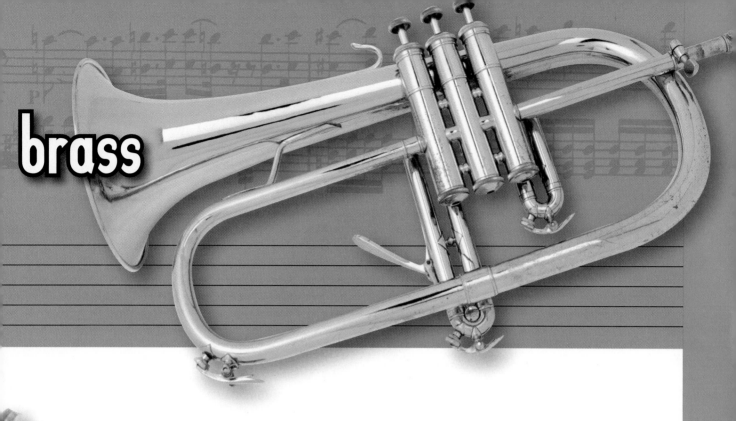

brass

The third section has brass instruments. The brass section is made up of horns. Most horns are made out of brass, a type of metal. Some of the brass instruments are the French horn, the trumpet, and the trombone.

Last is the percussion section. Percussion players strike their instruments. The kettledrum, snare drum, bass drum, and triangle are just some of the percussion instruments. The piano is also a percussion instrument.

percussion

Seating

One reason orchestra members sit or stand in certain places is because of how loud their instruments are.

Musicians in the strings section sit closest to the conductor. Their playing leads the orchestra's sound. They sit in pairs. Each pair reads the music on one stand. The strings are the largest section of an orchestra. They need to be heard over the brass and percussion instruments.

Musicians have page-turning partners. They work together to follow the sheet music.

Orchestra musicians are experts at playing their own types of instruments.

Members of the woodwinds, brass, and percussion sections do not share a music stand. They play different parts. So they have separate music stands. Most musicians who play percussion instruments stand in the back. They have some of the loudest instruments.

Each member of a section must collaborate with others to play well. Everyone must know when to play his or her part.

Orchestras Everywhere

Almost every country has an orchestra. Many places also have orchestras for children. Many schools have music programs.

Many children begin playing instruments when they are seven years old. Some children are even three years old when they start learning. Their instruments are small. But they look just like the larger instruments.

Some students try a few instruments before they discover their favorite instrument.

Professional and student orchestras spend hours perfecting the way they play music together.

Students begin by learning simple songs. The music teacher tells students to practice. This is the best way to get better.

The key to a successful orchestra is collaboration. The musicians must work together to make music. Each musician plays an important role. Each instrument has a unique sound. It is amazing to hear so many instruments blend into one beautiful sound. Which instrument would you like to play?

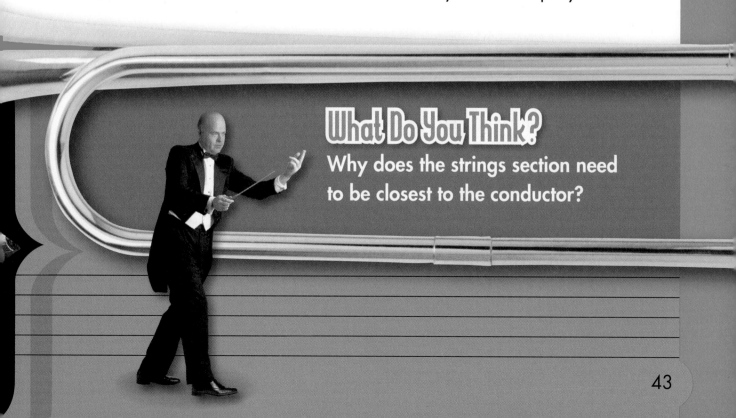

What Do You Think?

Why does the strings section need to be closest to the conductor?

MOLLY'S NEW ROLE

by Sara Jo Schwartz
illustrated by Kathy Couri

It was a big day for Molly. She was trying out for the new school play, *The Golden Merry-Go-Round.* She sang and danced. Three teachers and three students sat at the front of the auditorium. They would choose the actors.

"Good job, Molly," said Mr. Andrews after she read her lines. "Next!"

On Monday, the cast list appeared. Molly raced over to read it. Her name was not there.

"Molly," called Mr. Andrews. "Could you come here a minute?" he asked. "Molly, you have accomplished so much as an actor," Mr. Andrews said. "But this time we would like you to try something else. There are many other interesting jobs. Teamwork is what makes a play a real success."

Molly nodded. She left the room and ran home. Her grandmother was waiting. She looked at Molly's face. It reminded her of storm clouds.

45

"I didn't get a part in the play!" Molly cried. Then she told Grandma what Mr. Andrews said.

"You have a lot to think about, Molly," Grandma said.

Later, Molly called her friend. "Jessica, I'll just forget about the play," she said. "And I won't go to see it."

Jessica sounded disappointed. "Oh, Molly," she said. "Why don't you work on the scenery?" But Molly had already made up her mind.

46

Everyone in the auditorium was busy working on the play. Some students worked on posters or scenery. Other students would be in charge of the lights and sound. Some students had to open and close the curtain.

Jessica's group was in charge of gathering props. Props are the things on stage that make a play seem real. The stage had to look like a circus with a merry-go-round.

As the weeks passed, Molly's classmates accomplished so much for the play. After school, Molly just went straight home.

One night Jessica called. She told Molly about the merry-go-round horse she was making.

"It doesn't look real," Jessica complained.

Molly sat up. She knew where to find a real merry-go-round horse. Grandma's friend Mr. Cohen collected merry-go-round horses. She didn't tell Jessica this though. She had a lot to think about.

Molly found Grandma in the kitchen. She told her what had happened. "What do you want to do?" Grandma asked.

Molly smiled. "I want to cooperate."

Grandma smiled back. "Let's call Mr. Cohen."

Mr. Cohen was happy that someone was interested in his collection.

"Molly, I've got the perfect horse," he said. "It needs a little paint, but you can make it look good as new."

The next day, Molly's father brought the horse to the auditorium.

"This is a perfect prop!" Jessica exclaimed. "Will you help more?"

Molly had to admit she liked cooperating. "Sure! I'll work on props," she said.

She already had some great ideas. Looking for props was like going on a treasure hunt. The props group used teamwork to find what they needed.

50

Soon Molly felt as if she had been on the team all along. When Mr. Andrews came to take a look at the scenery, Molly was trying to move a tall ladder on the stage.

"Can you help us with this ladder?" she asked Mr. Andrews. "Remember what you told me about teamwork? It isn't just for students, you know!"

WHAT DO YOU THINK?
What has Molly learned as a member of the props group?

Winning Teams

In April, 1970, the *Apollo 13* space mission almost ended in disaster. The spaceship was damaged. Crew members were short of oxygen. The world watched and worried. The three men worked as a team to repair their ship. They used their training, and they remained calm. This helped them repair the ship. Five days later, the crew returned safely home. Now there is a movie about this heroic team.

Sometimes members of a team make history. They are not forgotten.

In 2005, the Chicago White Sox won the World Series. This was an amazing feat. They hadn't won a World Series since 1917! For many fans it seemed as if they would never win. The White Sox of 2005 had a lot of players determined to win. They played hard, they played smart, and they won.

The United States Women's Soccer team caught the attention of fans around the world in 1996 and 2004. This group of women showed their strength and teamwork during the Olympic games.

The young women played as a team to win two gold medals. They won gold medals at the 1996 and 2004 Olympics.

How could the American colonists living in the thirteen colonies become one united country?

In 1776, the U.S. colonists declared their independence from Britain. As a united group, they fought and won their freedom. Men, women, and children had to work as a team. Families helped feed the troops. And they helped deliver messages about British troops. Together, the colonists formed a new nation.

4 YOU 2 DO

Word Play

It's time to sign up for an after-school activity. Read the advertisement on the right. Then choose concept words that could be used instead of the underlined words or phrases.

Making Connections

It takes more than actors and musicians to put on plays and concerts. How do other jobs help make a performance successful?

On Paper

Do you have a skill or talent? Write about the ways you could help a team now or may help one in the future.

Is <u>cooperation</u> important to you?

Come Join the Art Club.

Every <u>person</u> will have fun!

All art projects require <u>working together</u>.

This year we have an art exhibit. We will show what we have <u>done</u> this year.

Possible answers for Word Play: collaboration, member, teamwork, accomplished

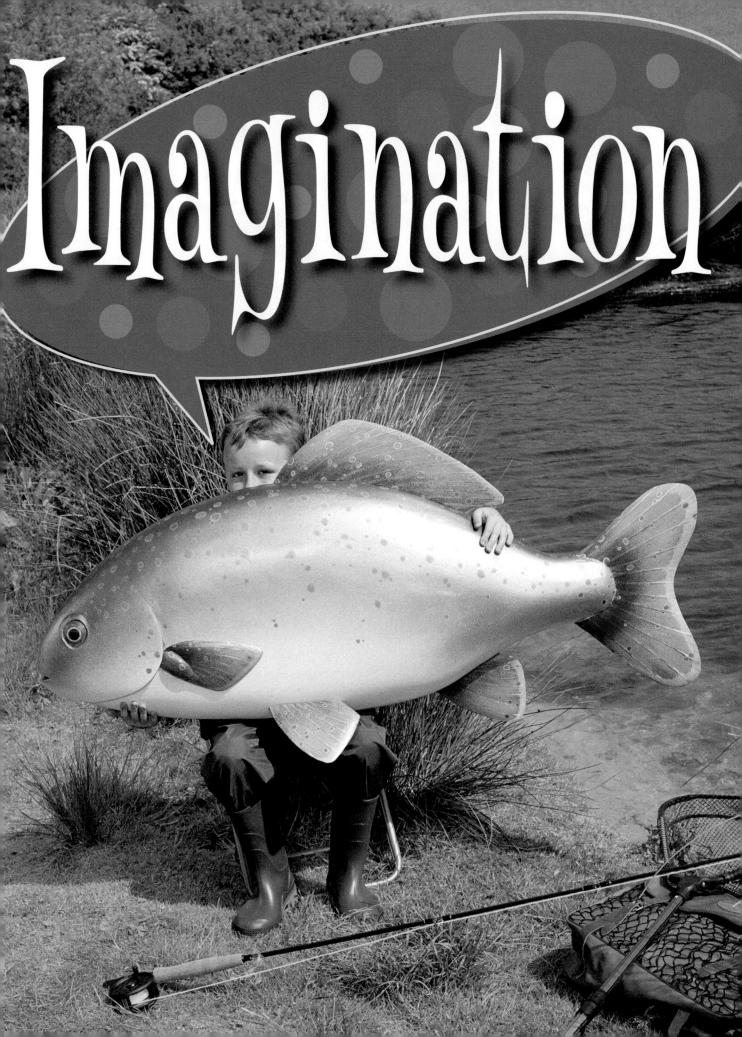

Contents

Imagination

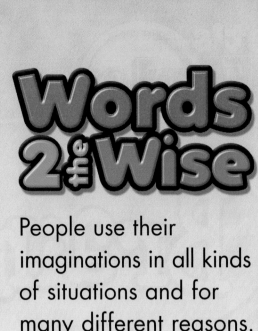

Words 2 the Wise

People use their imaginations in all kinds of situations and for many different reasons. As you read, think about the ways you use your **imagination.**

Let's Explore

Brainstorming

What can you imagine? That's up to you. You use your mind to brainstorm ideas. Brainstorming helps you come up with ideas that maybe nobody has ever thought of.

Writers use brainstorming all the time. They ask "what if" questions. "What if a storm comes?" "What if the lights go out?" Then, they make up exciting stories.

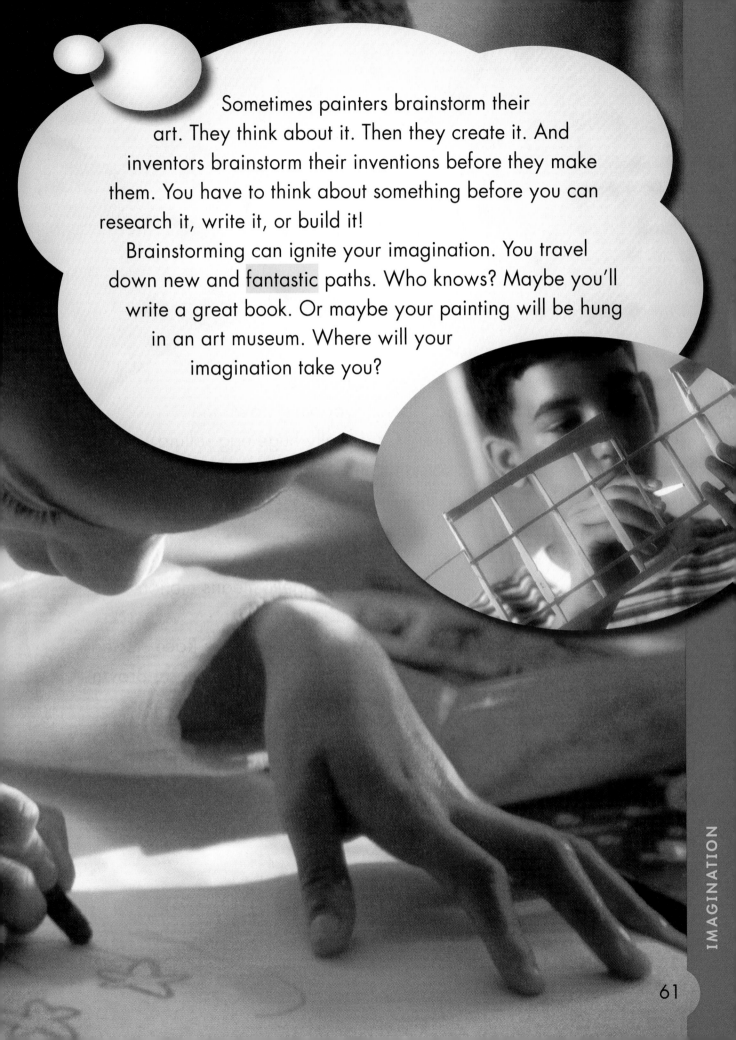

Sometimes painters brainstorm their art. They think about it. Then they create it. And inventors brainstorm their inventions before they make them. You have to think about something before you can research it, write it, or build it!

Brainstorming can ignite your imagination. You travel down new and fantastic paths. Who knows? Maybe you'll write a great book. Or maybe your painting will be hung in an art museum. Where will your imagination take you?

Racing Art

by Emma G. Rose

Hobart Brown rides his *Pentacycle*.

Have you ever seen a giant horse wobbling down the street? Or a really huge egg rolling down the street?

If you have, then you must have watched the Kinetic (ki-NET-ik) Sculpture Race. Imagine something rolling, wobbling, and swimming. *Kinetic* means motion. This race is art in motion!

The Kinetic Sculpture Race started in California in 1969. Hobart Brown made his son's three-wheeler more interesting. He added two more wheels. Then he made it seven feet tall.

He called his invention the *Pentacycle*. *Penta* means five. It had five wheels. It was very unusual.

Hobart's friend, Jack, wanted to build something even more unusual. He built a twelve-foot-tall army tank.

The two friends challenged each other to a race. Word spread about their contest. More artists entered. There were 14 sculptures on race day.

"I couldn't believe it," said Jack. He thought it was fantastic. So many people wanted to race.

This tank is twelve feet tall!

It's not unusual to see a dragon on race day.

The *Pink Elephant* raced in the 1999 race.

The race did not go well for Hobart. His *Pentacycle* crumpled. A giant tortoise won. It laid eggs and spit steam.

But everyone agreed. Racing sculptures was fun. They decided to race again.

The racers came from around the country. One invention was a wild dragster. Someone else made a giant flower. About ten thousand people watched.

More people competed every year. The silliest sculptures were a rubber duck and a pink elephant.

The *Pentacycle* and the *Tortoise* after the first race in 1969.

The scariest sculptures were an iguana and a dinosaur skeleton. The fanciest racer was *Bridle Trail.* It was a white horse. It had spots, long eyelashes, and angel wings.

The race takes three days. Racers travel 42 miles. The sculptures race over roads of sand and mud. They also float on water.

The racers are made from spare parts. They use lawn mowers, bicycles, and car parts! They decorate their machines with feathers, tinfoil, and paper.

In 2003, *Bridle Trail* won the art award.

Some sculptures have one driver. Others have a group of drivers. There are about 38 rules for racing.

Here are some basic rules.

1. All sculptures must be people-powered.
2. Drivers' feet can't touch the ground.
3. Sculptures can have up to five drivers.
4. Sculptures must pass a safety test. They must have working brakes and lights.
5. Sculptures can be up to eight feet wide and 14 feet high. But they can be long as you want! No length is too fantastic.

The *Two-Ton Tricycle* was built for three riders.

Some of the rules are really silly.
One silly rule is that sixth graders can be
members of a team, but not as drivers. And
the silliest is that each racer must carry
a teddy bear. The last rule explains
the inspiration behind the race.
You have to have fun!

Surf 'n' Turf is a
bull and an octopus
riding on a lobster

67

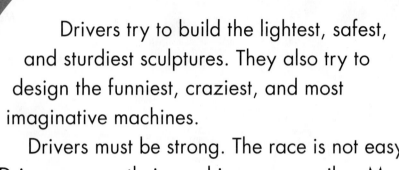

Drivers try to build the lightest, safest, and sturdiest sculptures. They also try to design the funniest, craziest, and most imaginative machines.

Drivers must be strong. The race is not easy. Drivers power their machines many miles. Most drivers don't care about finishing first. They just care about finishing without pushing. One driver said, "Anyone can fix up a ten-speed bike and go fast. My idea is to go funny."

Al the Albino Rhino won the Grand Champion in 2003.

Pilots, wearing their life preservers, steer the giant red-eyed tree frog sculpture *Croak* across the water.

There are all kinds of winners in this race. The most colorful sculpture gets the Art Award. The best floating and moving sculpture gets the Engineering Award. The Speed Award goes to the fastest machine. The sculpture with the highest total points becomes the Grand Champion.

The Kinetic Sculpture Race mixes art, inspiration, and science. Winning means being imaginative and having fun.

What Do You Think?

Why isn't being first to cross the finish line most important?

SAM AND THE INCREDIBLE SMASH

BY JEFF O'KELLEY
ILLUSTRATED BY GARRY COLBY

Captain X-TRA sprang into action!

Professor Smash's atomic ray was blasting all over the city. Cars exploded and buildings crashed with each blast!

"My puppy!" a woman yelled. A puppy was sitting in the street. It was about to be crushed by a falling building!

Captain X-TRA flew down in a flash. He snatched the dog just before the building smashed to the ground.

"Oh, thank you, Captain X-TRA," the woman cried.

"All in a day's work, ma'am," said Captain X-TRA.

Professor Smash had to be stopped!

Captain X-TRA flew towards the park to find him. People cheered.

"Save us!"

"Take me with you!"

"You're extraordinary, Captain X-TRA!"

At the park, Professor Smash protected his atomic ray. His eyes were wide with madness. "Nothing can stop me!" he screamed. "Nothing!"

A large rock rested next to Captain X-TRA. Could he get it past Professor Smash? He would try his hardest.

One skillful kick should do it.

"Just kick the ball!" Coach yelled.

Sam stood in front of the soccer ball. The goalie was waiting for him to kick.

"All right, Professor Smash," he whispered to himself. Sam got ready.

It was too late. Another player took a shot. Then another. They were tired of waiting. Sam had done it again. He had missed his chance.

The members of both teams were already finished warming up and the game was about to begin.

The rest of the team went out on the field. Sam took a seat on the bench. Coach stood next to him as the game started.

"Watch Ted," Coach told Sam. "He's a skillful passer. He stays focused. You should learn that."

"Right," Sam said. He nodded slowly. "What did you just say?"

"Sam!"

"Just kidding," Sam laughed.

"I'm going to put you on the field," Coach said. "Be ready. Stay focused."

"Okay," Sam said.

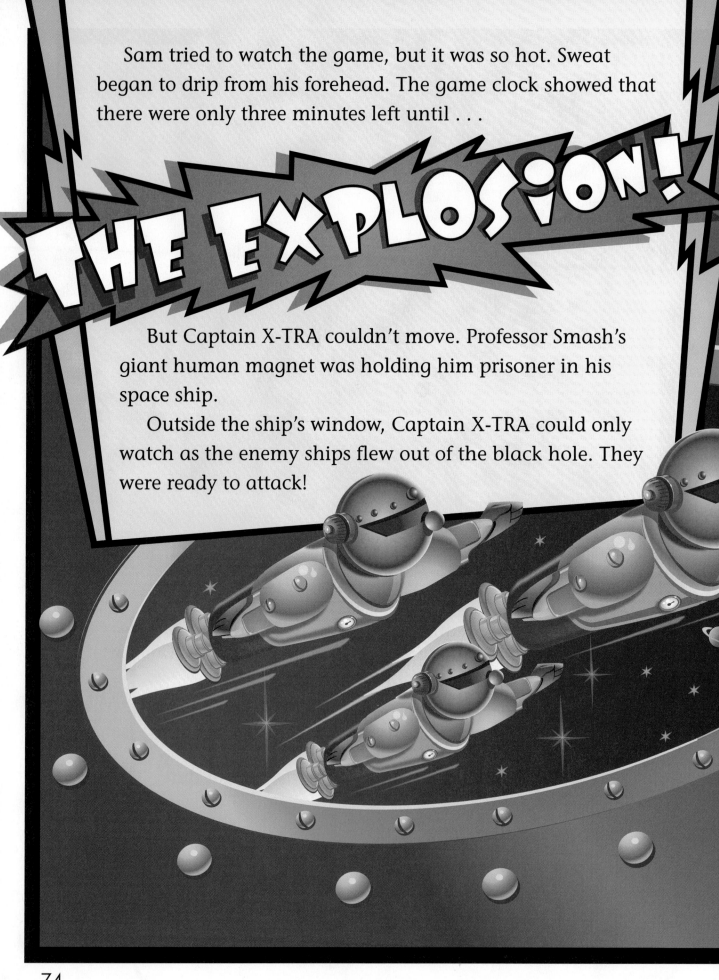

Sam tried to watch the game, but it was so hot. Sweat began to drip from his forehead. The game clock showed that there were only three minutes left until . . .

THE EXPLOSION!

But Captain X-TRA couldn't move. Professor Smash's giant human magnet was holding him prisoner in his space ship.

Outside the ship's window, Captain X-TRA could only watch as the enemy ships flew out of the black hole. They were ready to attack!

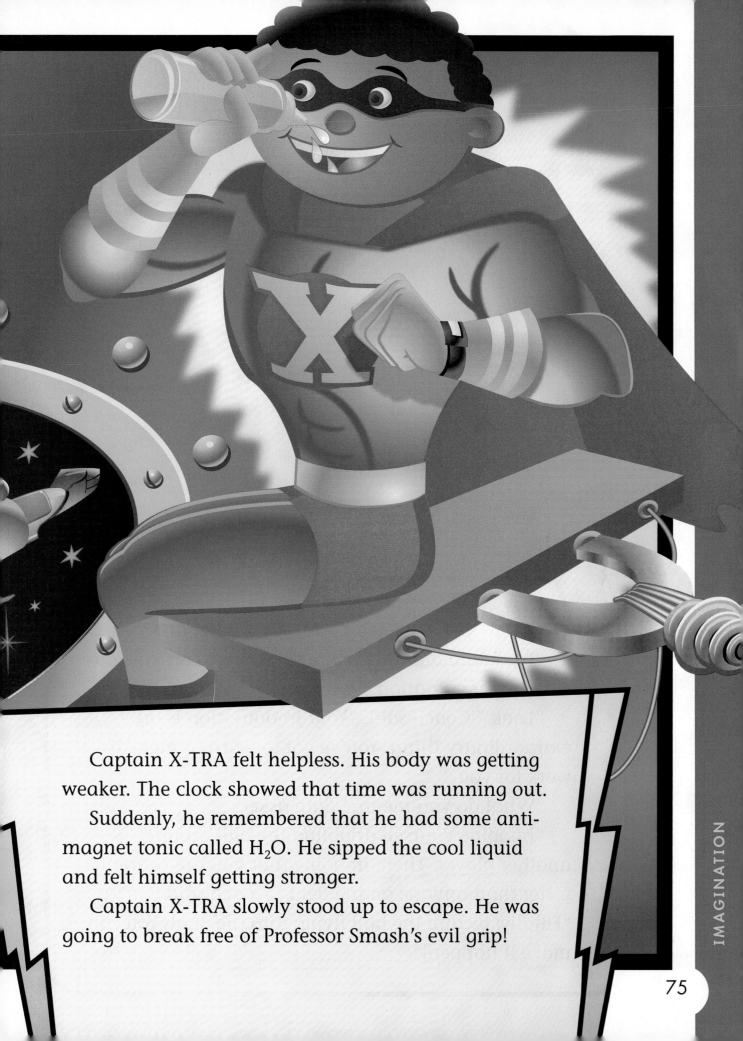

Captain X-TRA felt helpless. His body was getting weaker. The clock showed that time was running out.

Suddenly, he remembered that he had some anti-magnet tonic called H_2O. He sipped the cool liquid and felt himself getting stronger.

Captain X-TRA slowly stood up to escape. He was going to break free of Professor Smash's evil grip!

"Sam!" Coach yelled. "Are you paying attention?"

"No," Sam admitted. "I'm sorry. I get carried away with my imagination."

"Look," Coach said. "Your imagination is an extraordinary thing. You've got to learn to make it work for you."

"What do you mean?" Sam asked.

"Imagine yourself dribbling the ball around another player. Then, imagine that you are running faster than anyone on the field," Coach said. "Finally, picture the ball flying into the goal. You can make it happen!"

"Right!" Sam said.

"Good. Now get in there!" Coach shouted.

Sam's team moved the ball toward the goal. Sam found himself in position to score.

The ball came to him. Now it was just Sam and the goalie. Sam pictured the ball going into the net. *Steady, steady,* he thought.

And then he smashed the ball into the goal!

"There you go!" Coach yelled.

Sam grinned. Maybe his imagination wasn't so bad after all.

WHAT DO YOU THINK?

How did Sam's imagination help him score a goal?

LIVING THE HIGH LIFE

Have you ever built a tree house? You can see a lot from high up in a tree. But would you want to sleep in one? Some people do!

Grown-ups and kids can "nest" for a night in a tree house resort in Washington. This tree house is 50 feet above the ground. The tree trunk grows straight up through the kitchen.

This observation area is connected to the tree house hotel by a rope suspension bridge.

The state of Oregon has tree house resorts too. One resort has 18 tree houses. They are built in oak trees. Swinging rope bridges connect the houses. The highest tree house is 37 feet above ground. One of the tree houses, called the Suite, has a bathroom with a shower. It even has a small kitchen with a refrigerator and a microwave.

This tree house complex has a trap door and a fire pole you can slide down to the ground on!

A swinging rope bridge connects the rooms at this tree house.

One of the biggest tree houses in the world is the tree house in Northumberland, England. Visitors can shop and eat at a restaurant in this tree house. Kids of all ages can use its suspended walkways to explore.

This tree house in England is the biggest in the world.

Visitors to the tree house can warm up next to the log fire inside!

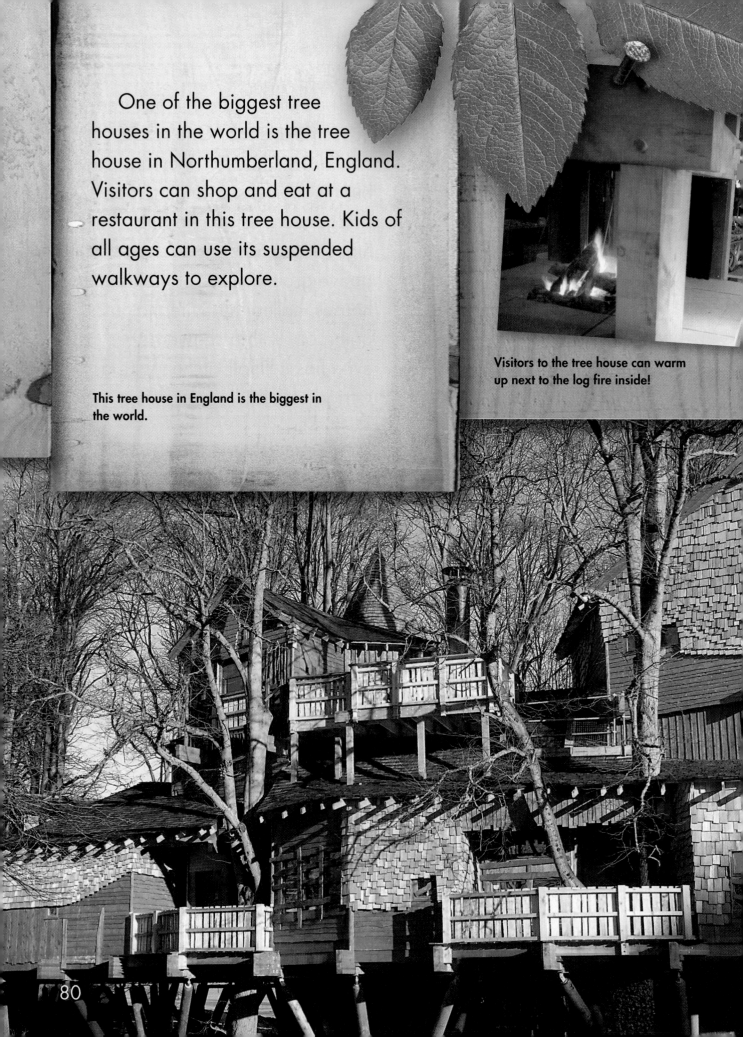

In a tree house, nature is your neighbor. Birds and squirrels scamper from branch to branch. Bridges and walkways let people move from branch to branch too.

Tree houses are fun places to play and sleep. But they can also be good places to learn about the natural world around you.

This tree house in England features above-ground walkways and bridges.

4 you 2 Do

Word Play

How many words can you see within these words? Find at least 3 words of 3 letters or more in each word.

extraordinary

inspiration

fantastic

Making Connections

What can happen when people use their imaginations? Use examples from the readings and what you already know to answer.

On Paper

Describe an idea or activity that you brainstormed. What does it look like? How does it work? What is it for?

Contents

A JOB WELL DONE

Let's Explore

Words 2 the Wise

You might not be familiar with many jobs. As you read, think about the different jobs people do. What does it mean when someone says, "That's a **job well done**"?

Let's Explore

Everyday Jobs

Think of someone famous. What is this person famous for? Is it the work he or she does for a living?

We often admire people with exciting or glamorous jobs. Their lives are always in the spotlight. We may even daydream about doing what they do.

But many people have jobs that we hardly ever notice. They are not in the spotlight. They are collecting our garbage. They are stocking food on our store shelves. They are making our roads safer. They are teaching us to read. There are thousands of everyday jobs that make our lives easier and better.

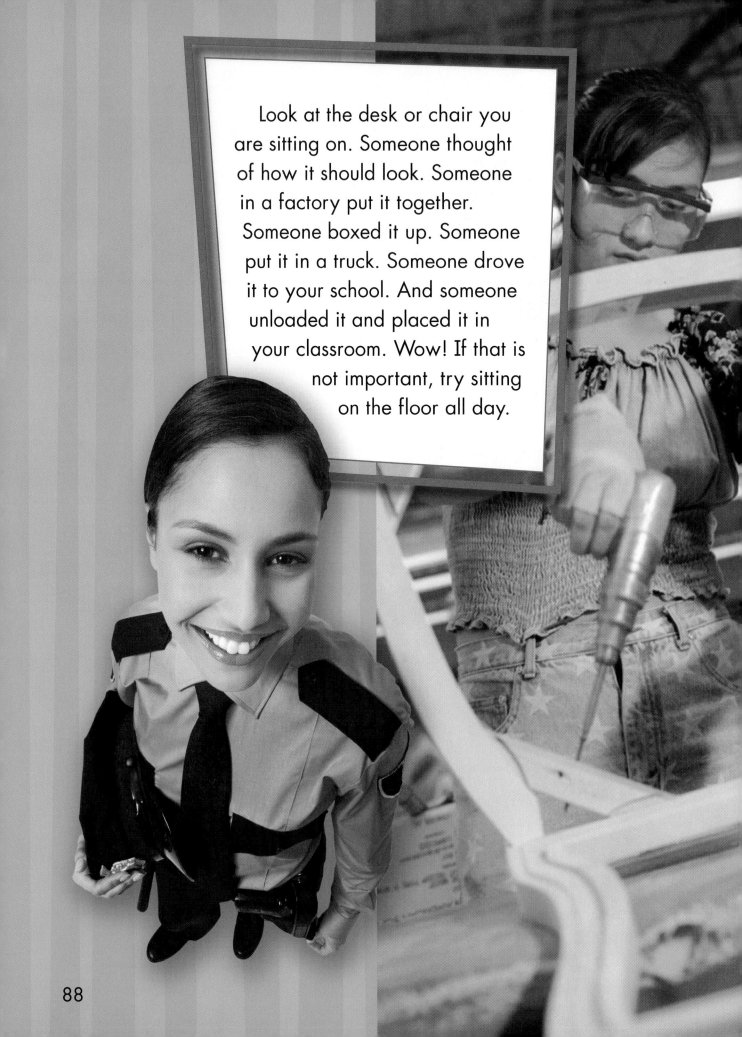

Look at the desk or chair you are sitting on. Someone thought of how it should look. Someone in a factory put it together. Someone boxed it up. Someone put it in a truck. Someone drove it to your school. And someone unloaded it and placed it in your classroom. Wow! If that is not important, try sitting on the floor all day.

Thousands of jobs like these affect our everyday lives. The people who do these jobs may never be in the news. But they are important. Look around you. Can you think of any jobs that get done without your knowing?

THE BIG DIG

OF BOSTON

BY JAMES DIXON

IN A GIANT JAM

For years, Boston had a terrible traffic problem. Its old, elevated highway was not wide enough. And it was falling apart. Cars and trucks jammed its lanes. Traffic crawled into and out of Boston. The highway made one straight route through the city. People had a hard time getting to some areas.

The old highway in Boston was always full of traffic.

City planners knew these problems would grow. They worried people might not want to seek a new career or spend free time in Boston. So, they came up with a big plan—the Big Dig!

The Big Dig would create a new highway. People were amazed when they read about the plans. Workers would build many miles of tunnels. Some tunnels would go underwater. They would replace the old highway.

A model of downtown Boston was built to plan for the Big Dig.

Above: Work had to continue without shutting down highways or railroads.

Work on the Big Dig could not shut down the city. That wasn't an option. The old highway had to stay open. So did train tracks and subways.

THE SUPER SCOOP

The Big Dig project started with an underwater tunnel. It would be 50 feet under Boston Harbor. What could dig so deep? The Super Scoop could!

The Super Scoop sat on a huge, table-shaped boat that moved very slowly across the harbor. The Scoop worked nonstop to dig up rocks and mud for almost a mile. It took two years to finish this part of the first tunnel.

The first tunnel was finished in 1995. But workers had much more to do.

Right: Workers pieced together tubes that were as long as a football field.

Below: The Super Scoop worked night and day.

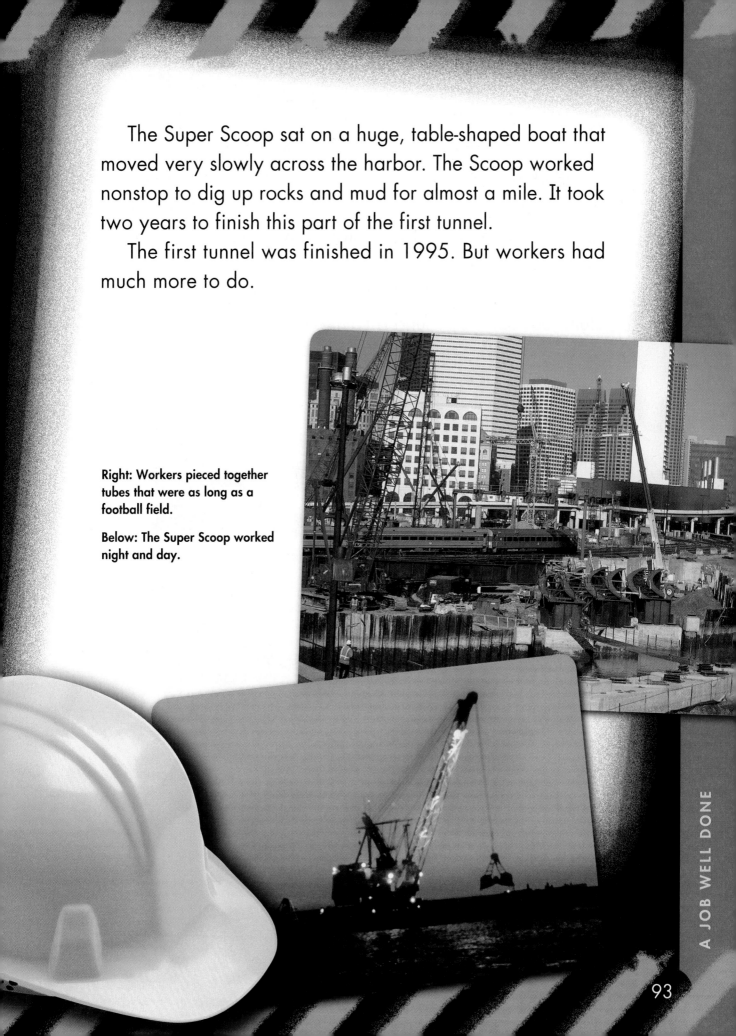

93

A TUNNEL WITH LEGS

Work soon began on a second underwater tunnel. But there was a problem. A big problem. Another tunnel was already down there. The Boston subway ran through it.

The highway tunnel couldn't sit on top of the subway tunnel. It would crush it. Even experienced builders were stumped. But they found a solution.

This machine drilled deep holes in the earth.

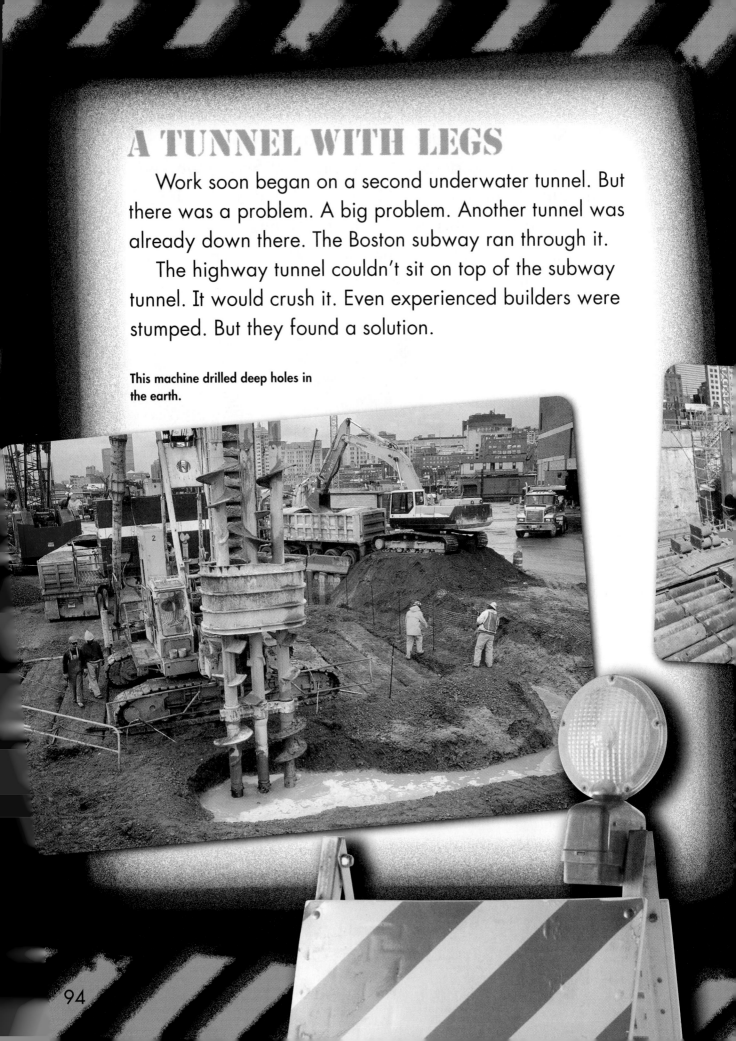

The new tunnel would have legs! Workers placed a row of columns along each side of the subway tunnel. Then they rested sections of the highway tunnel on top of the columns. Caps on each section fit tightly over the columns.

Today, the new highway tunnel is a busy place. Traffic moves quickly below the surface. A huge, new bridge also stretches above.

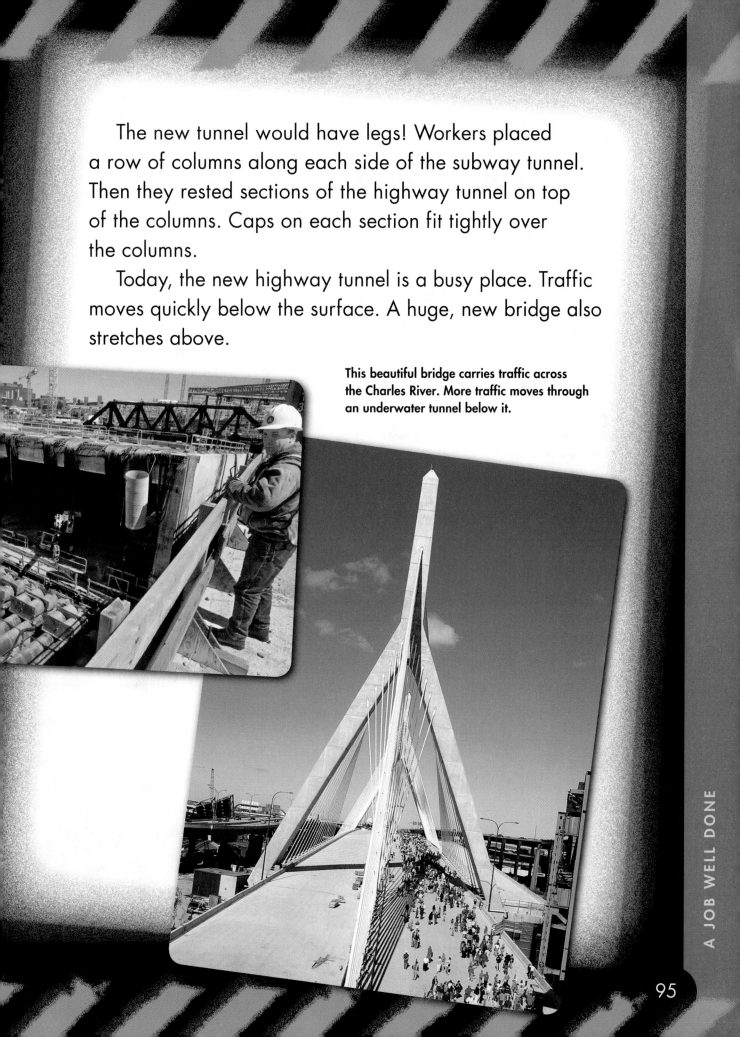

This beautiful bridge carries traffic across the Charles River. More traffic moves through an underwater tunnel below it.

PUSH POWER

Big Dig workers also built tunnels under railroad tracks. Digging under the tracks wasn't a safe option. But pushing was.

Big Dig workers would dig like a worm does. They built a giant tunnel box called the "worm." Powerful machines shoved the "worm" forward. This made a path. It was slow going. Workers cleared only about nine feet of dirt each day.

This machine works like a worm. It "eats" dirt as it moves forward.

Workers had to knock down old columns to build new ones.

HIT THE HIGHWAY

Builders also planned another tunnel. This one would go under the old elevated highway. Columns holding up the old highway were in the tunnel's path. So workers built new columns. Then they knocked down the old ones.

In 2004, the new highway was finished. Planning and building the Big Dig took several years. Many people with different careers were involved. It took big efforts to make the Big Dig.

WHAT DO YOU THINK?
Which tunnel was built first? Which tunnel was built next?

All the Right Moves

by Michelle Schaub   illustrated by Jim Steck

Rob rushed home after school. He dropped his backpack by the sofa. Then he searched for his skateboarding gear. *What was it doing under the sofa?* Rob grabbed it and left. He wanted to hit the skate park before dark.

Rob loved skateboarding. If he had the option, he would skate morning, noon, and night. Rob's twin sister Rosie was good on the ramps too. She had been waiting for him.

"Let's roll!" said Rosie.

The twins' mom shook her head. "So much for their chores," she sighed.

Rob and Rosie each had a daily job. Rosie had to load and unload the dishwasher. Rob had to clean up the family room. Both jobs made good sense. Rob always dumped his stuff in the family room rather than put it away. Rosie left dishes everywhere.

The twins came home just before dinner. All they could talk about was their friend Jamie.

"You should see Jamie's skateboard ramp, Dad!" said Rob.

The twins had been begging their dad to build them a skate ramp. So far, he'd said no. Still, they watched him hopefully now. But Dad just frowned. He'd seen Rob drop his gear in the family room. He'd watched Rosie set her empty glass on the bookshelf.

Rob's mom walked in. She frowned too.

"Rob, it looks like a tornado came through here," she said. "And Rosie, I see dirty dishes everywhere. This is a family room, not a kitchen!"

"We'll clean later," said the twins. "We have homework." Of course, they had to find their schoolbooks first.

Rob and Rosie didn't get far before they ran out of energy. They fell asleep before they had a chance to clean up.

The next day Rob came home with an armful of papers. He went to find Rosie. She was in the kitchen, unloading the dishwasher.

Rob spread the papers on the table. "Rosie, check this out."

Rosie saw drawings and measurements. They were plans for a skateboard ramp.

Rosie whistled. "How did you get these?"

"I borrowed the plans from Jamie. He and his dad don't need them now that their ramp is done," said Rob.

"What's the point," Rosie groaned. "Dad will just say no."

"We have to prove how much we want this," said Rob. "We need to start doing our chores and our homework without Mom having to bug us."

"We could also give Dad our saved up birthday money," said Rosie. "That will be our contribution towards the cost of the ramp."

Rob looked at the cluttered family room. "This is going to be tough," he said.

"If we want that skateboard ramp, we better get busy cleaning," Rosie said.

Rosie put away all the dishes. Then she began to search the house. She checked under beds, along windowsills, and behind furniture. Forgotten glasses, cups, and plates piled up.

After dinner, Rosie loaded the dishwasher. Then, they did their homework. Finally, they decided it was time to ask again.

"Notice anything different?" Rob asked.

Dad raised his eyebrows. "Let's see. You did your jobs. You even had energy left over for homework. Is this because of the skateboard ramp?"

The twins grinned.

"We promise to do our chores and our homework. If we don't, you can take down the ramp," Rob explained. "We'll also give you our birthday money as a contribution."

"That's a fair option," said Mom. "What is it you kids say? Let's roll!"

What Do You Think?

How do Rosie and Rob reach their goal?

Why Do We Work?

People work to earn money, of course. But there are other reasons that people work. Some reasons don't have anything to do with money!

You can help people whether it's your job or something you volunteer to do. Teaching others can be fun too.

Some people work at jobs that started as a hobby. Do you like to take care of animals, explore the outdoors, or paint? These fun activities could someday be your job.

Your love of painting could turn into a full-time job!

What makes someone a good swimming teacher?

Is this work or fun? For people who like nature, the answer is both!

Great Job!

How can you do a good job?

Artists, musicians, and dancers practice to get better.

1. Plan Ahead

Know what you have to do. Take a big job and break it into smaller steps. Plan how much time you'll need. Write a list of materials.

2. Take Action with a Good Attitude

Having a positive attitude makes any job easier! Try to enjoy yourself, even if parts of the job aren't fun.

3. Get It Done

Keep working on the job until it is finished. Congratulate yourself when you've completed a challenging task!

Word Play

A wind storm has scrambled the words on these signs! Your job as a signmaker is to fix them. Place the letters in the right order to spell each vocabulary word.

noiptso

aceerr

tbsnioncoriut

Making Connections

What do you think Rob and Rosie could learn from the workers who helped with the Big Dig in Boston? Explain your answer.

On Paper

Is your town or neighborhood in need of a big or small project? Would it improve life for people in your area? Describe a project in your neighborhood or tell about one that the town needs.

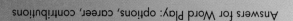
Answers for Word Play: options, career, contributions

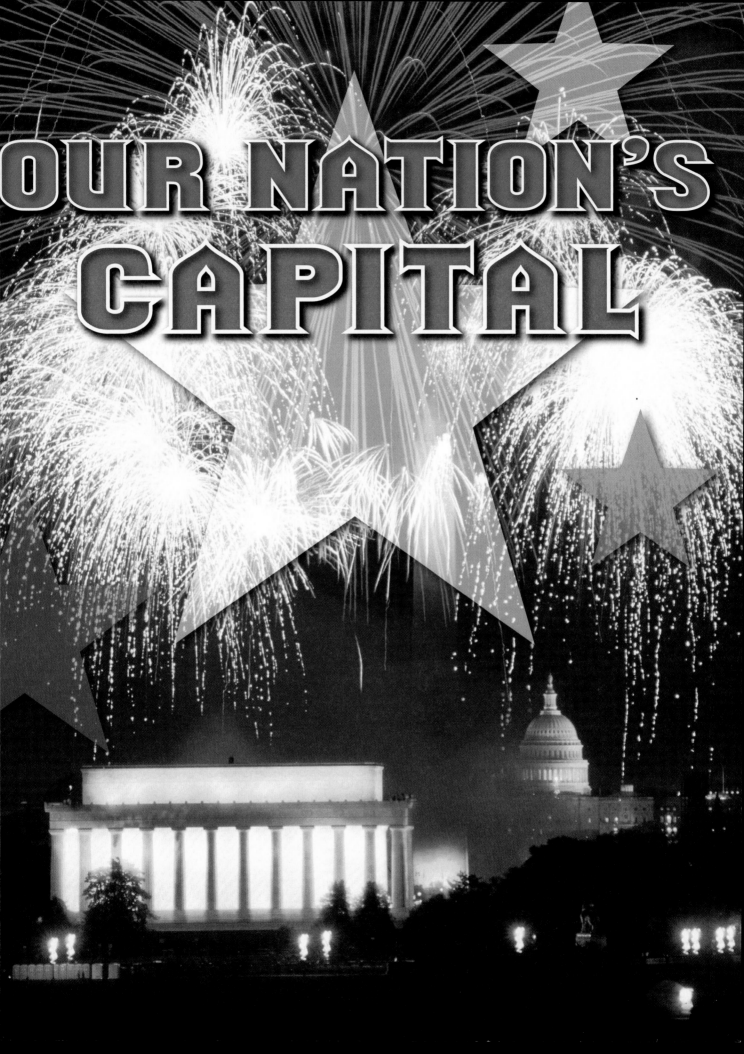

Contents

OUR NATION'S CAPITAL

Choose an activity and explore this week's concept—Our Nation's Capital.

Words 2 the Wise

Our nation's capital has a long and interesting history. There are many fascinating buildings, stories, and people. As you read, think of questions you have about our capital.

Let's Explore

Birth
—of the—
Capital

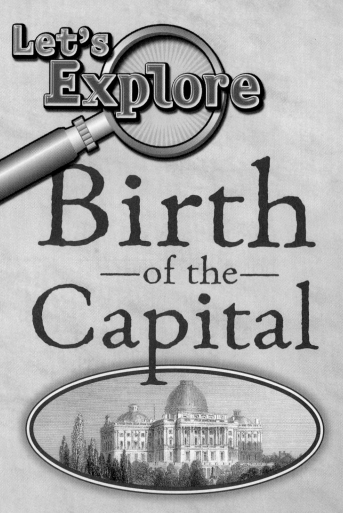

Did you know that Washington, D.C., wasn't our nation's first capital? New York and Philadelphia were the first capitals. People from the South thought these cities were too far north. They wanted the capital to be close to both the North and the South.

President George Washington chose the new spot in 1791. The capital city would be on the Potomac River between Virginia and Maryland. It was in the center of the thirteen states.

Washington hired Pierre L'Enfant (pyair lohn-FOHN) to help design the capital. He planned for the capital buildings to be built around the White House. But after one year, L'Enfant was fired. Then Benjamin Banneker was hired to finish the capital.

President Washington helped plan the city. So it seems right that *Washington* is part of its name. And the *D.C.* stands for "District of Columbia" after Christopher Columbus. Welcome to our nation's capital!

Benjamin Banneker (left) was hired to finish the plans for Washington, D.C. (above).

Working in the
White House

by Dennis Fertig

The White House is a famous home. We call it the Executive Mansion. An executive is someone who runs a government or business. The President is our chief executive. He leads our country. The White House is also his home. His family lives there.

The White House is different from most homes. It is the center of activity in our capital. The White House is large. It welcomes many guests.

Some White House jobs are done only for the President. These jobs are exciting. Why? Because they help make important decisions!

But the first family also needs help to keep the White House running smoothly. They get help from many talented people.

Cristeta Comerford has the honor of being the first female chef in the White House.

White House Chef

The White House chef has an important job. The chef has a staff of two full-time cooks. During one recent month the chef served 9,500 meals at 26 different events!

The White House chef had always been a man. First Lady Laura Bush changed that in 2005. She hired the first woman chef. Her name is Cristeta Comerford.

Some White House guests come from the nearby Capitol building. Some come from distant countries. The chef feeds them all.

Chief Usher

What is an usher? Is it a person who works in a theater? In the White House the Chief Usher makes sure everyone is doing his or her job.

The Chief Usher runs a staff of 95 people. This staff includes chefs, butlers, and maids. They make sure the President's family and guests are comfortable. The staff also includes carpenters, electricians, and plumbers. They keep the White House in good repair.

Gary Walters (left) has been the Chief Usher since 1986. The man on his right is his assistant.

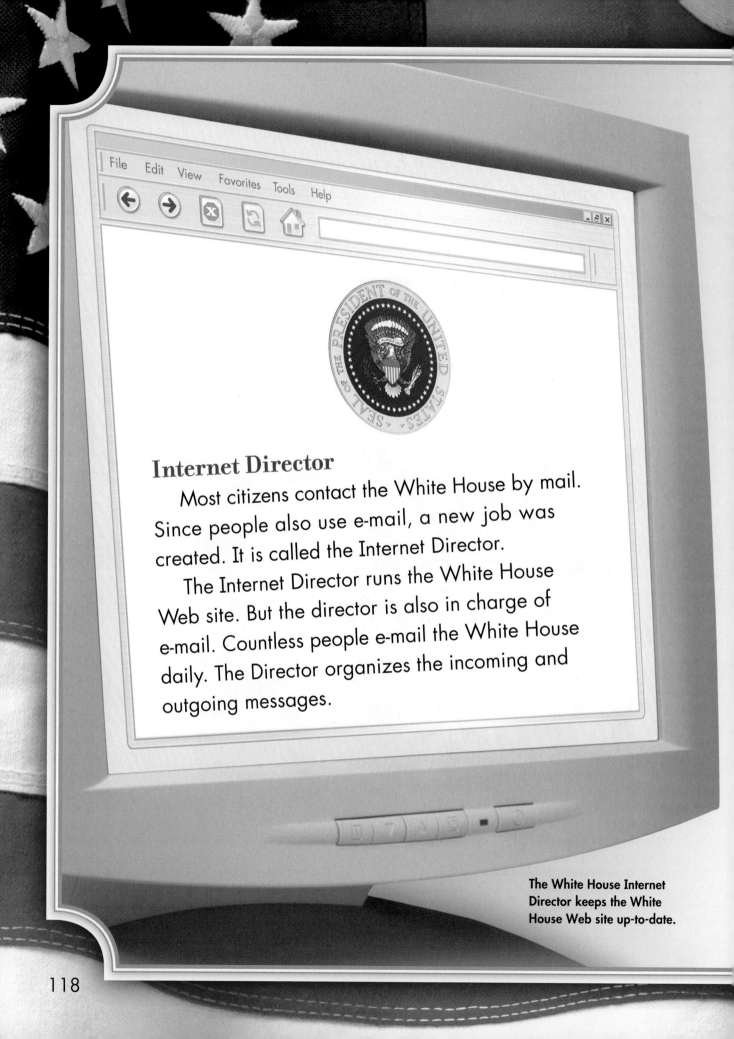

Internet Director

Most citizens contact the White House by mail. Since people also use e-mail, a new job was created. It is called the Internet Director.

The Internet Director runs the White House Web site. But the director is also in charge of e-mail. Countless people e-mail the White House daily. The Director organizes the incoming and outgoing messages.

The White House Internet Director keeps the White House Web site up-to-date.

President Bush greets a group of children. Can you find the Secret Service agents in the crowd?

White House Guard

Secret Service agents are always near the President. They also protect the first family.

The Secret Service also protects the White House and other buildings in the capital. Uniformed agents patrol on foot, bikes, motorcycles, or in cars.

The Secret Service checks every visitor to the White House, even people from the nearby Capitol building.

Do you want to tour the White House? Agents will check you too.

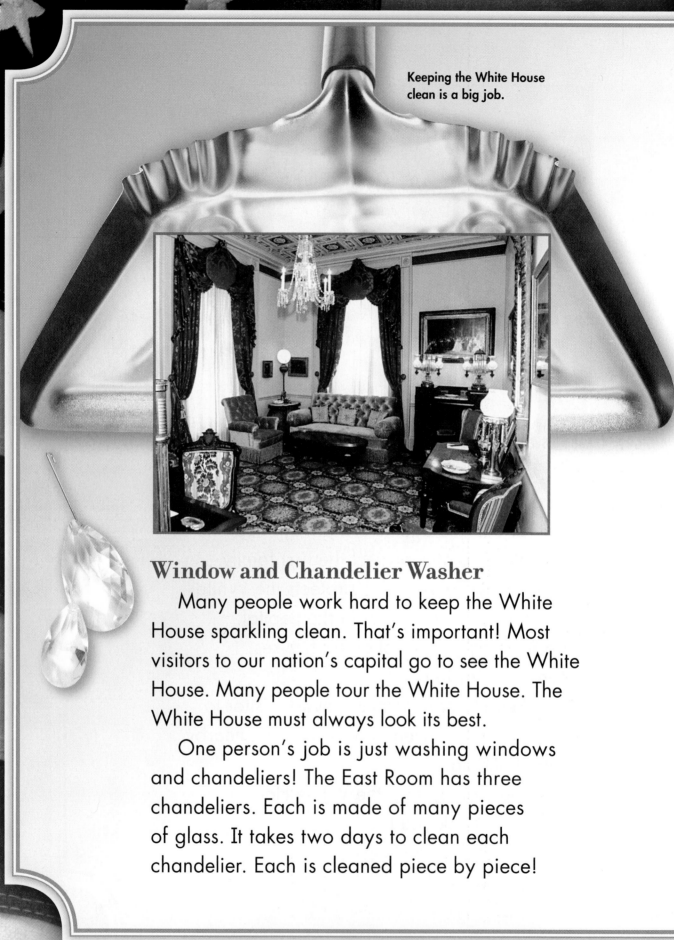

Keeping the White House clean is a big job.

Window and Chandelier Washer

Many people work hard to keep the White House sparkling clean. That's important! Most visitors to our nation's capital go to see the White House. Many people tour the White House. The White House must always look its best.

One person's job is just washing windows and chandeliers! The East Room has three chandeliers. Each is made of many pieces of glass. It takes two days to clean each chandelier. Each is cleaned piece by piece!

120

There are many jobs in the White House. The work is hard. Yet most people keep their jobs for a long time. Why? The White House is a wonderful place to work! They help make people proud of the most important house in America.

Do you want to write to the White House?

The White House
1600 Pennsylvania Avenue NW
Washington, DC   20500

What Do You Think?
Why is it important for White House employees to do a good job?

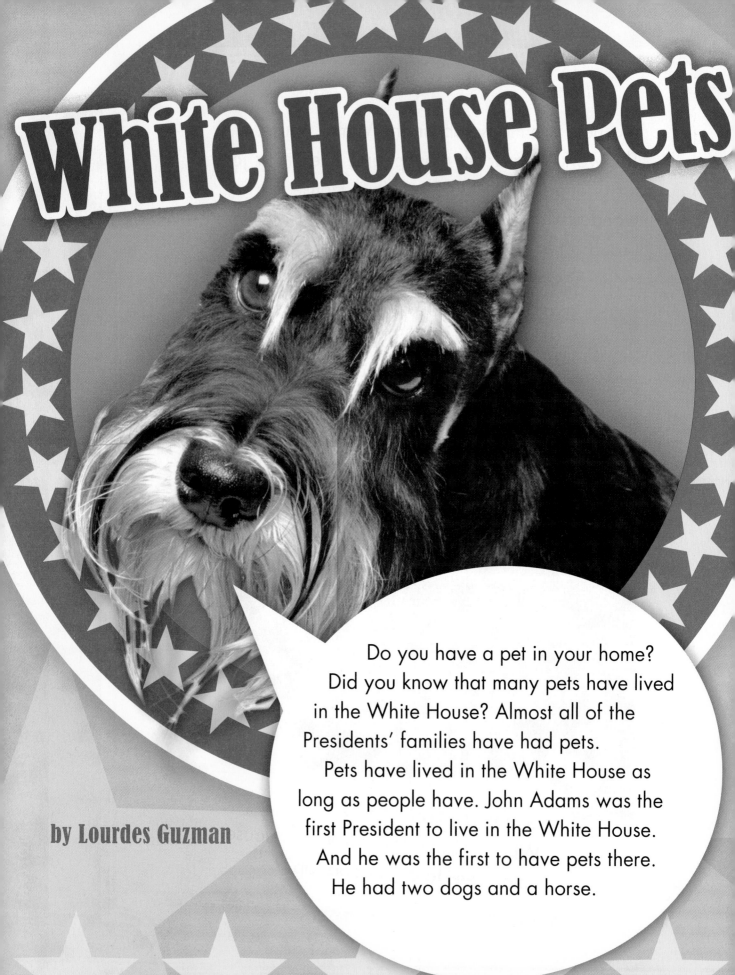

White House Pets

by Lourdes Guzman

Do you have a pet in your home? Did you know that many pets have lived in the White House? Almost all of the Presidents' families have had pets.

Pets have lived in the White House as long as people have. John Adams was the first President to live in the White House. And he was the first to have pets there. He had two dogs and a horse.

All kinds of pets have lived at the White House. The list is surprisingly long. There have been many dogs and cats. But there have also been some unusual pets. There have been parrots, elephants, and sheep. There have been tigers, goats and alligators. More than 400 pets have lived in the Executive Mansion!

President Kennedy's children, Caroline and John, had a pony.

Which President had the most pets? Teddy Roosevelt had the most. He had a big family. He let his children have a lot of pets. He also loved to ride horses. Some of his pets are listed below.

President Roosevelt's son once let four snakes loose in the White House. Some of the White House guests ran away in fear!

President Roosevelt's Pets

dogs	bears	
cats	rats	
coyote	lion	guinea pigs
owl	hyena	wildcat
zebra	lizard	raccoon

Calvin Coolidge had a lot of pets too. He had many of the same pets that Teddy Roosevelt had. But President Coolidge also had a hippo and a wallaby. He was famous for walking his pet raccoon! Could you imagine a President walking a raccoon? President Coolidge loved pets. He thought that a person who didn't have pets shouldn't be President!

Below Left: President Hoover named his dog after a famous Egyptian. It was called King Tut.

Below Right: First Lady Grace Coolidge holds Rebecca, the pet raccoon.

Tiger was a tabby alley cat that belonged to President Coolidge.

One day President Coolidge's favorite cat disappeared. The President asked radio stations for help. He wanted people to help look for his cat.

There is also a funny story about President Benjamin Harrison. He had a pet goat named Whiskers. Whiskers often pulled a cart around the White House lawn. The President's grandchildren liked to ride in the cart.

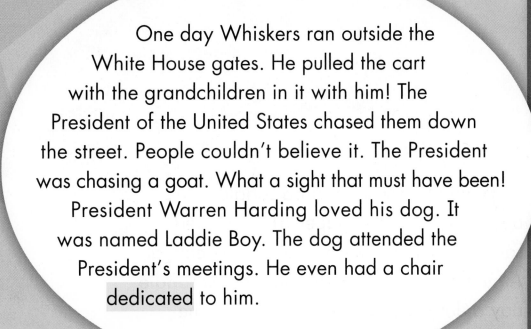

One day Whiskers ran outside the White House gates. He pulled the cart with the grandchildren in it with him! The President of the United States chased them down the street. People couldn't believe it. The President was chasing a goat. What a sight that must have been! President Warren Harding loved his dog. It was named Laddie Boy. The dog attended the President's meetings. He even had a chair dedicated to him.

A newspaper once hired Laddie Boy to write for the paper. They wanted Laddie Boy to write about life in the capital. A human really wrote the stories. But Laddie Boy did have a real birthday party. The President invited other dogs. They enjoyed dog-biscuit cake!

Recent first families have had popular pets too. President Reagan owned a dog named Rex. And President Clinton had a cat named Socks and a dog named Buddy.

President George W. Bush's dog
Barney stars in many videos.

People enjoy learning about White House pets. There is even a museum that is dedicated to White House pets! The Presidential Pet Museum displays memorabilia of the White House pets. Some of the memorabilia includes photos, newspaper articles, and t-shirts! There are over 500 items in the museum. People learn about the Presidents when they learn about their pets.

What Do You Think?

Why do people like hearing about White House pets?

Washington's Wonderful Monuments

There are many interesting parks, museums, monuments, and buildings that are worth visiting in Washington, D.C.

United States Capitol

The Capitol is the first place to visit. Congress makes laws here. If you get a chance, watch Congress at work.

The Capitol will surprise you. It's huge. And it's filled with wonderful bits of history!

This is a view of the dome inside the Capitol.

Washington Monument

Stand on the Capitol's front steps and you'll see the Washington Monument. What a sight! No building in Washington, D.C. is taller. And since the monument honors our first President, no building should be.

The impressive Washington Monument is 555 feet tall and weighs 90,854 tons.

Lincoln Memorial

Can a statue leave you breathless? The giant statue of Abraham Lincoln in this memorial might. Lincoln seems to gaze right down on you. You have to see our nation's tribute to this brave President!

Inside the Lincoln Memorial is a 175-ton statue of President Abraham Lincoln.

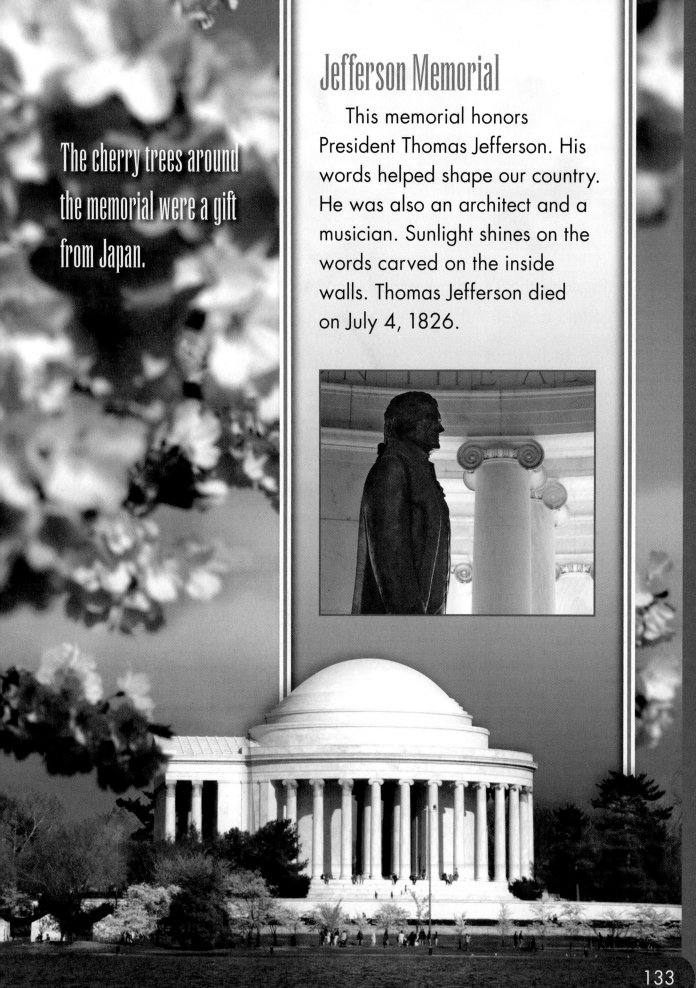

The cherry trees around the memorial were a gift from Japan.

Jefferson Memorial

This memorial honors President Thomas Jefferson. His words helped shape our country. He was also an architect and a musician. Sunlight shines on the words carved on the inside walls. Thomas Jefferson died on July 4, 1826.

4 YOU 2 DO

Word Play

Replace the Xs below with the correct letters to spell this week's vocabulary words.

xedxcatxd

capxxal

xapixxl

mxmoxabixia

xusxum

Making Connections

Pretend you have only one morning to visit Washington, D.C. Which place would you tour? Why?

On Paper

Think about the White House jobs you read about. Which one would you like to do? Why?

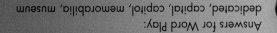

Glossary

ac·com·plish (ə kom′ plish), *VERB.* to complete; carry out: *She accomplished more today than anyone else.* *VERB* **ac·com·plished, ac·com·plish·ing.**

a·ware·ness (ə wâr′ ness), *NOUN.* knowledge; act of realizing: *It's important to have an awareness of what's going on around you.*

cap·i·tal (kap′ ə təl), *NOUN.* a city where the government of a country or state is located; where laws are made: *Washington, D.C., is the capital of the United States.*

Cap·i·tol (kap′ ə təl), *NOUN.* 1. the building in Washington, D.C., in which Congress meets: *We took a tour of the Capitol building in Washington, D.C.* 2. also, capitol, the building in which a state legislature meets: *The state representatives met in the capitol to discuss many important laws.* *USAGE NOTE:* Capitol and capital are often confused. *Capitol* is a building. The Capitol stands in Washington, D.C. *Capital* is a city.

ca·reer (kə rir′), *NOUN.* an occupation or a profession:
I plan to make teaching my career.

col·lab·o·ra·tion (kə lab ə rā′ shen), *NOUN.* working
together to get something done: *Our collaboration on
a report on whales received an A.*

com·pre·hend (kom′ pri hend′), *VERB.* to understand
something: *If you can use a word correctly, you
comprehend it. VERB* **com·pre·hend·ed,
com·pre·hend·ing.**

a	in hat	ō	in open	sh	in she
ā	in age	ȯ	in all	th	in thin
â	in care	ô	in order	₮H	in then
ä	in far	oi	in oil	zh	in measure
e	in let	ou	in out	ə	= a in about
ē	in equal	u	in cup	ə	= e in taken
ėr	in term	u̇	in put	ə	= i in pencil
i	in it	ü	in rule	ə	= o in lemon
ī	in ice	ch	in child	ə	= u in circus
o	in hot	ng	in long		

con·tri·bu·tion (kon′ trə byü′ shen), NOUN. money, help, advice that is given; gift: *The famous actor made a generous contribution to his favorite charity.*

co·op·e·rate (kō op′ ə rāt′), VERB. to work together: *Everyone cooperated in helping to clean up after the class party.* VERB **co·op·e·rat·ed, co·op·e·ra·ting.**

ded·i·cate (ded′ ə kāt), VERB. to set something apart for a purpose: *The author chose to dedicate her first book to her parents.* VERB **ded·i·cat·ed, ded·i·cat·ing.**

en·er·gy (en′ ər jē), NOUN. strength; the power to work, move or play: *She has so much energy when she plays basketball.* NOUN PL. **en·er·gies.**

ex·ec·u·tive (eg zek′ yə tiv), NOUN. 1. someone who manages a business, a department of a government, and so on: *The president of a company is the top executive.* 2. ADJECTIVE. having the duty and power of putting laws into effect: *As the executive leader of the country, the President approves new laws.*

ex·hi·bit (eg zib′ it), *NOUN.* public showing or display: *The students went to the museum to see the new exhibit about space.*

ex·per·i·ence (ek spir′ ē əns), *NOUN.* 1. events that are seen, done, or lived through: *People learn by experience.* 2. knowledge or skill gained by seeing, doing, or living: *I've gained valuable experience from working with computers.*

a in hat	ō in open	sh in she
ā in age	ȯ in all	th in thin
â in care	ô in order	ŦH in then
ä in far	oi in oil	zh in measure
e in let	ou in out	ə = a in about
ē in equal	u in cup	ə = e in taken
ėr in term	ù in put	ə = i in pencil
i in it	ü in rule	ə = o in lemon
ī in ice	ch in child	ə = u in circus
o in hot	ng in long	

ex·traor·di·nar·y (ek strôr′ də ner′ ē), *ADJECTIVE.* very unusual; remarkable; special: *Eight feet is an extraordinary height for a human being.*

fan·tas·tic (fan tas′ tik), *ADJECTIVE.* causing wonder or surprise: *The audience cheered loudly after the fantastic magic show ended.*

gear (gir), *NOUN.* the equipment needed for some purpose: *They packed a flashlight, a tent, a compass, and other gear needed for their camping trip.*

ho·ri·zon (hə rī′ zn), *NOUN.* range of one's thinking, experience, interest, or outlook: *She took an art class to expand her horizons.*

in·spi·ra·tion (in′ spə rā′ shən), *NOUN.* 1. something that has a strong effect on what you feel or do, especially something good: *The science fiction author got inspiration from the books she read.* 2. a sudden, brilliant idea: *The artist's unexpected inspiration changed the way she painted forever.*

in·ter·ac·tive (in′ tər ak′ tiv), *ADJECTIVE.* allowing a person to use more than one sense to learn something: *Most computer games are interactive.*

mem·ber (mem′ bər), *NOUN.* a person, animal, or thing belonging to a group: *He is a member of the drama club.*

mem·or·a·bil·i·a (mem′ ər ə bēl′ ē a), *NOUN.* things or events saved for remembering: *I have memorabilia from my childhood in my scrapbook.*

a	in hat	ō	in open	sh	in she
ā	in age	ȯ	in all	th	in thin
â	in care	ô	in order	ŦH	in then
ä	in far	oi	in oil	zh	in measure
e	in let	ou	in out	ə	= a in about
ē	in equal	u	in cup	ə	= e in taken
ėr	in term	u̇	in put	ə	= i in pencil
i	in it	ü	in rule	ə	= o in lemon
ī	in ice	ch	in child	ə	= u in circus
o	in hot	ng	in long		

mu·se·um (myü zē′ əm), *NOUN.* a building for displaying a collection of objects related to science, ancient life, art, or other subjects: *I like to visit the science museum.*

op·tion (op′ shən), *NOUN.* something that can be chosen; a choice: *Recess is not an option in many schools.*

or·ches·tra (ôr′ kə strə), *NOUN.* a group of musicians playing strings, brass, woodwinds, and percussion instruments. An orchestra is usually led by a conductor. *NOUN PL.* **or·ches·tras.**

sculp·ture (skulp′ chər), *NOUN.* a piece of art made from stone, wood, clay, or other things: *She created a sculpture of a famous writer.*

skill·ful (skil′ fəl), *ADJECTIVE.* having ability, knowledge, or experience: *He is very skillful at painting houses.*

team·work (tēm′ wėrk′), *NOUN.* People working together to be successful at something: *It takes teamwork to win a tug-of-war.*

work·er (wėr′ kər), *NOUN.* someone who does a job: *Jim is an excellent worker.*

a	in hat	ō	in open	sh	in she
ā	in age	ȯ	in all	th	in thin
â	in care	ô	in order	ŦH	in then
ä	in far	oi	in oil	zh	in measure
e	in let	ou	in out	ə	= a in about
ē	in equal	u	in cup	ə	= e in taken
ėr	in term	u̇	in put	ə	= i in pencil
i	in it	ü	in rule	ə	= o in lemon
ī	in ice	ch	in child	ə	= u in circus
o	in hot	ng	in long		

Acknowledgments

Illustrations

20–27 Jeff Mangiat; **45–50** Kathy Couri; **70–77** Garry Colby; **98–105** Jim Steck

Photographs

Every effort has been made to secure permission and provide appropriate credit for photographic material. The publisher deeply regrets any omission and pledges to correct errors called to its attention in subsequent editions.

Unless otherwise acknowledged, all photographs are the property of Scott Foresman, a division of Pearson Education.

Photo locators denoted as follows: Top (T), Center (C), Bottom (B), Left (L), Right (R), Background (Bkgd).

Opener: (CR) ©Windsor & Wiehahn/Getty Images, (L) Stockdisc, (T, B) Getty Images, (L) Rubberball Productions, (BR) ©Smiley N. Pool/Dallas Morning News/Corbis; **1** Rubberball Productions; **2** (TR) Stockdisc, (C) Getty Images; **3** (TR) Randall Frost/©Humboldt Kinetic Association, (C) Stockdisc, (BR) ©Steven Peters/Getty Images; **5** ©Philip Gatward/Alamy Images; **8** Getty Images; **9** (T, BC) Getty Images; **10** (B) ©Bill Bachmann/Index Stock Imagery, (TCL) Getty Images; **11** Brand X Pictures; **12** (T, CC) Getty Images, (BC) NASA Image Exchange; **13** (TL) ©Museum of Science, Boston, (TR, CR) Getty Images; **14** (BR) Comstock Images, (BL) Getty Images, (CL) ©Discovery Place; **15** (TL, TC, BL, BR) PhotoSpin, (TR) ©Richard Cummins/Corbis; **16** (TL) ©Stanley Smith/Experience Music Project, (CL, BR) Getty Images; **17** (B) ©David Young Wolff/PhotoEdit, (BR, CC, T) Getty Images; **18** (T, C, CL) Getty Images; **19** Getty Images; **28** ©David Crausby/Alamy; **29** (TL) Creatas, (BC) ©Junko Kimura/Getty Images; **30** ©Justin Pumfrey/Getty Images; **31** ©Hans Neleman/Getty Images; **34** (R) Getty Images, (CL) ©David R. Frazier Photolibrary, Inc./Alamy Images; **35** ©Tom Mackie/Getty Images; **36** (T) Lebrecht Collection, (BR) Getty Images; **37** (B) ©Chad Ehlers/Stock Connection, (TL) Getty Images; **38** (T) Design Pics, (BCL, BR) Getty Images; **39** (T, BR) Getty Images, (B) ©Odile Noel/Lebrecht Collection; **40** (T) Getty Images, (B) ©Mooncoin/Alamy; **41** (T) Comstock Images, (CR) Jupiter Images; **42** (TC) Getty Images, (B) ©Lawrence Migdale; **43** (T) ©John L. Russell/AP Images, (BC, BL) Getty Images; **52** (L) Marshall Space Flight Center/NASA Image Exchange, (TCR) NASA Image Exchange; **53** (C) ©John G. Mabanglo/Corbis, (TR) Getty Images; **54** (C) ©Smiley N. Pool/Dallas Morning News/Corbis, (TL) Getty Images; **55** (C) ©Dennis McDonald/PhotoEdit, (B) Geoff Brightling/Courtesy of the Order of the Black Prince/©DK Images, (BR) Getty Images; **56** Stockdisc; **57** ©Windsor & Wiehahn/Getty Images; **59** ©Ingram Publishing/SuperStock; **60** ©Garfield Hall/Getty Images; **61** ©Richard Heinzen/SuperStock; **62** Randall Frost/©Humboldt Kinetic Association; **63** (B, TR) Randall Frost/©Humboldt Kinetic Association; **64** (BR) ©Jon Meyers/MoonRay Imaging, (BR) ©Layne Kennedy/Corbis; **65** ©Jon Meyers/MoonRay Imaging; **66** ©Jon Meyers/MoonRay Imaging; **67** (BR) ©Jon Meyers/MoonRay Imaging, (TC) ©Duane Flatmo; **68** ©Jon Meyers/MoonRay Imaging; **69** (TL, BL) ©Jon Meyers/MoonRay Imaging; **78** (R, BC) ©Bill Compher/Cedar Creek Treehouse, (TR, R) Getty Images; **79** (CL, BR) ©Michael Garnier/Treesort and Treehouse Institute of Takilma, OR; **80** (B, TR) © The Alnwick Garden, (T) Getty Images; **81** (C, BR) ©The Alnwick Garden, (BC) ©Royalty-Free/Corbis; **82** Creatas; **83** Stockdisc; **86** (CL) Getty Images, (R) ©Bettmann/Corbis; **87** (BL) Stockdisc, (R) ©Royalty-Free/Corbis; **88** (BL) Stockdisc, (T) ©Marc Asnin/Corbis; **89** (TL) Stockdisc, (R) ©Masterfile Royalty-Free; **90** (BR) ©Frank Siteman/Index Stock Imagery, (TL, C) Getty Images; **91** ©Steven Senne/AP Images; **92** (T) ©Ed Quinn/Corbis, (CR) ©Steven Senne/AP Images; **93** (CR) ©Adrian Greeman/Construction Photography, (B) Courtesy of the Massachusetts Turnpike Authority, (BL) Getty Images; **94** (C) ©Adrian Greeman/Construction Photography, (B) Getty Images; **95** (CL) ©Steven Senne/AP Images, (BR) ©Michael Dwyer/AP Images; **96** ©Adrian Greeman/Construction Photography; **97** (T) ©Michael Dwyer/AP Images, (TL) ©Chitose Suzuki/AP Images; **106** (BL) ©Ron Yue/Alamy Images, (BR) BananaStock/SuperStock, (TL) ©Frances Roberts/Alamy Images; **107** (C, TR, BR) Getty Images; **108** Getty Images; **109** ©Timothy Murphy/Getty Images; **112** (TL) ©Bettmann/Corbis, (R) SuperStock; **113** (CR) "Benjamin Banneker Stamp" ©1980 United States Postal Service. Used with permission. All rights reserved. Written authorization for the Postal Service is required to use, reproduce, post, transmit, distribute, or publicly display these images./The Granger Collection, NY, (BR) Geography and Map Division/Library of Congress, (BC) Getty Images; **114** (C) PhotoDisc, (CC) ©MediaImages/Getty Images; **116** (Bkgd) PhotoDisc, (TC) ©Tina Hager/White House/Getty Images, (C) Getty Images; **117** ©Dennis Cook/AP Images; **118** (Bkgd) PhotoDisc, (C) Getty Images; **119** (TC) ©Tim Sloan/AFP/Getty Images, (TCR) Getty Images; **120** (Bkgd) PhotoDisc, (TC) ©Mark Viker/Getty Images, (CC) ©Liaison/Getty Images; **121** ©Royalty-Free/Corbis; **122** Getty Images; **123** (TR) Getty Images, (BR) ©John F. Kennedy Library/Getty Images; **124** (L, CC, BR, BC) Getty Images; **125** (BR) ©Royalty-Free/Corbis, (CC) ©Herbert E. French/Corbis, (CR) National Photo Company Collection/Library of Congress; **126** (L) Getty Images, (CR) Herbert E. French/Library of Congress; **127** Getty Images; **128** (BL, R) Getty Images; **129** (TL) ©Paul Mors/Getty Images, Getty Images; **130** (B) Getty Images, (CR) Brand X Pictures; **131** (C, CR) Getty Images; **132** Getty Images; **133** (C) ©Matthew Cavanaugh/epa/Corbis, (CR) Getty Images; **134** ©Steven Peters/Getty Images; **136** Jupiter Images; **137** Getty Images; **138** ©FogStock/Index Open; **139** Getty Images; **140** ©Photos Select/Index Open; **141** ©Jacque Denzer Parker/Index Open; **142** Brand X Pictures; **143** Brand X Pictures

144